My Best Fiend

'My best friend is called Angela Mitchell and she lives in the house next door.' There is nothing unusual about this opening description Charlie Ellis gives of her best friend, but the tales which follow reveal the very unusual scrapes these two friends seem to get in to.

The scrapes always begin with Angela having marvellous ideas which mean disaster, especially for Charlie who always seems to get the blame when Angela's so-called marvellous ideas go horribly wrong! Like the time Angela forced Charlie to cut short Angela's beautiful long hair so that she would get the part of Prince Charming in the school play. Angela did get the part, but not until a hairdresser had put right the results of Charlie's catastrophic scissor-work! But it is Charlie's own sense of loyalty and generosity towards her friend Angela that ends in Angela unwittingly getting the come-uppance she deserves.

SHEILA LAVELLE

My
Best Fiend

Illustrated by Linda Burch

FONTANA · LIONS

First published in Great Britain 1979 by
Hamish Hamilton Children's Books Ltd
First published in Fontana Lions 1980
by William Collins Sons & Co Ltd
14 St James's Place, London SW1
Third impression July 1984

Copyright © 1979 Sheila Lavelle

Reproduced, printed and bound in Great Britain by
Hazell Watson & Viney Ltd,
Member of the BPCC Group,
Aylesbury, Bucks

I

MY best friend is called Angela Mitchell and she lives in the house next door. When she was three years old Angela painted the cat green. She wanted to make it look pretty, only after a few days all the cat's fur fell out and it went completely bald. Angela's mum had to knit it a little woolly coat to wear until its fur grew back again.

I'm allowed to call Angela's mum Auntie Sally because they live next door, and she often comes in for a cup of tea in the afternoons with my mum. They have long cosy chats together with their elbows on the kitchen table, and I like to listen because Auntie Sally is always talking about the funny things Angela did when she was little. Like the time when she was only two and she put a tin of black bootpolish in the washing machine and ruined all her dad's shirts and underwear. And another time when she was four and she poured treacle into her grandad's wellingtons. My mum and Auntie Sally giggle into their teacups and say what a little rascal, did you ever see a child like it, and gaze fondly at Angela's golden hair.

If you saw Angela you would understand why I think she must be the prettiest girl in the whole world. To start with she has this lovely long golden hair that tumbles down over her shoulders and is cut in a thick fringe at the front. She's got big blue eyes like cornflowers and great long eyelashes, and rosy cheeks that dimple when she smiles which is nearly all the time. She looks as though she couldn't be naughty if she tried. Not like me.

I'm sort of tall and thin and I've got brown eyes and short black curly hair a bit like a poodle. I've got long legs and I can run faster than Angela and my dad says I'm twice as bright as she is, but sometimes I wish I was as pretty. When she grows up Angela is going to be a queen.

'You can't be that,' I said scornfully when she told me. 'You can't be a queen when you grow up like you can be an actress or a dancer. The only way you can get to be a queen when you grow up is if your dad is a king!'

'Knickers!' retorted Angela rudely. 'You can still be a queen when you grow up, even if your dad is a plumber. You can MARRY a king! And then all your children would be princes and princesses, and you'd be rich!'

She's quite right of course. I hadn't thought of that. But I still don't like the idea much. There aren't all that many kings around to choose from, and anyway I'd rather marry someone like Kevin Keegan or Elton John. And then all my children would be footballers or pop stars and everybody knows they've got more money than kings and queens. In any case I prefer that nice man who reads the news on the telly. He's got a kind face just like my dad.

Although Angela is my best friend and she lives next door and we go everywhere together, we're not allowed to sit together at school. Miss Bennett, that's our teacher, won't let us. She says I'm a bad influence on Angela, and I bring out the worst in her, and she makes Angela sit two rows behind. When I told my dad about it he said it was a crying shame and that it was more likely the other way round. But I think he was just being on my side. Dads are nearly always on their daughter's side, have you noticed? It makes my mum a bit cross sometimes, especially when my dad lets me off helping with the washing up.

'You always take her part,' she complains, and my dad says 'Why not? Nobody else seems to stick up for the poor little . . .' and my mum says 'Ted!' in a sharp voice and then my dad doesn't say anything more.

Anyway, in class Angela has to sit next to that awful Delilah Jones who pinches you all the time, and I have to sit beside a big fat bully called Laurence Parker who's such a pudding that nobody could be a bad influence on *him*. All he cares about is eating, and teasing the little ones in the playground. He's as fat as a pig, and his pockets are always bulging with sweets because his father owns a sweet factory. You might think I'm lucky to sit next to a boy whose father owns a sweet factory, but it's not true. Laurence Parker eats them all himself because he's too greedy to give any away. Nobody likes him except Miss Bennett, and he brings her an enormous box of chocolates, all tied up with pink ribbon, at the end of every term.

But even though we don't sit together everybody knows that Angela is my best friend. One afternoon dur-

3

ing Creative Writing we all had to write a composition called 'Man's Best Friend'. When Miss Bennett told us the title I somehow didn't realize what she meant. I thought she must mean 'My Best Friend', so I wrote that down at the top of my paper and hoped it was all right. Miss Bennett promised to read the best composition out loud at the end of the lesson and I was hoping she'd choose mine. Because of course I wrote about Angela and I couldn't wait to see her face when she heard all the nice things I'd said about her.

I like writing compositions. You get a lovely clean sheet of paper and a nice newly-sharpened pencil and the paper has blue lines across it and one red line down the side called the margin and you're not allowed to write on the left of it. And it's ever so peaceful and quiet with everbody working away and thinking hard and Miss Bennett moving around the room looking over your shoulder and giving the slower ones a hand with the spelling. I'm a quick writer, and I had almost filled the page when Miss Bennett reminded us of the time.

'Only five minutes left, children,' she said. 'It's time some of you got a move on. I see that Angela Mitchell has so far only managed a couple of lines.'

I wasn't very happy when I heard that. It must mean either that Angela couldn't make up her mind who her best friend was, or that I was such a boring sort of person that she couldn't think of anything to say about me. I peeped round at her, but she was scowling at Miss Bennett and didn't look at me.

I got on with my work and then all at once a folded scrap of paper whizzed over my shoulder from behind and landed on my desk in front of me. Laurence Parker made a sort of hissing noise and I covered the paper quickly with my hand while he glared at me disapprovingly. I looked round at David Watkins who sits in the

4

desk behind mine but he shook his head and jerked his thumb in Angela's direction. Angela winked at me, and poked out her tongue at Miss Bennett who was at the front of the room with her back to the class.

I slid the paper off my desk and into my lap. If there's anything that Miss Bennett hates it's people passing notes during lessons. It makes her crosser than anything. There's always a big row if anybody gets caught doing it, but I still had to open Angela's note. I couldn't help it.

I unfolded the paper in my lap and my face went all sort of hot as I read it. It was in big sprawling capital letters and this is what it said.

MISS BENNETT IS A FOOL

I was still staring at it with my mouth open when Miss Bennett's voice made me jump.

'Charlotte Ellis!' she snapped. 'What are you doing? What's that in your lap?'

Miss Bennett is the only person who calls me Charlotte. Everybody else calls me Charlie and I like it much better. I think Charlotte's a soppy name. It makes you think of some kind of pudding.

When Miss Bennett shouted at me I got that nasty trickly feeling at the bottom of my stomach that you get when you know that something awful is about to happen. I inched up the lid of my desk and quickly pushed the note through the gap. Then I stood up. There's a rule in our class that you must always stand up if you want to speak to the teacher.

'Nothing, Miss Bennett,' I said, quite truthfully.

'Charlotte! I know perfectly well that you had something a minute ago,' said Miss Bennett. 'Please bring whatever it was out here to me this instant!'

There was no point in trying to hide the note if Miss Bennett had already seen it. But I couldn't let her read it. Angela would be in terrible trouble and Miss Bennett would never forgive her. What could I do? I opened my desk, thinking as hard as I could.

The note was lying, still open, on top of the books in my desk. I looked at it again. And then I suddenly saw that there *was* something I could do. I grabbed a pencil, and while I pretended to scrabble about looking for the note, I quickly added a few more letters to it. Then I crumpled it up in my hand and walked slowly out to the front of the class.

There was one of those dead silences in the room while everybody waited to see what would happen. Isn't it funny how people always love to see other people getting into trouble? I suppose it's because they're so relieved it isn't them. They had all stopped working and were nudging one another and staring. I didn't dare look at Angela.

Miss Bennett frowned at me as she took the note from my hand. She smoothed out the wrinkles in it and adjusted her glasses on her nose. Then she began to read. But as she read what the note said her face changed from a scowl to a pleased little smile and her cheeks grew pink. She looked round at the hushed class and I stole a quick look at Angela. She was staring at the ceiling with her best couldn't-care-less expression.

Miss Bennett cleared her throat. 'You all know how much I disapprove of passing notes in class,' she said. 'But this one says such a kind thing that I really don't think I can be cross about it.' And she held up the note for the class to see. This is what it said now.

MISS BENNETT IS
BEAUTIFOOL

I don't think anbody could have said that about Miss Bennett before. She's not too bad as a teacher, and she has lovely grey eyes and a nice kind face when she isn't being cross, but she just isn't beautiful and that's a fact. Some people are, and some people aren't, and there's not much anybody can do about it, I suppose. But Miss Bennett looked so pleased that I felt all sort of warm inside, and when I looked at her smiling like that with her face all pink, for a minute she really was quite beautiful.

A big sigh went all round the room like the wind in the treetops. One of the boys sniggered, but he managed to turn it into a sort of cough. Miss Bennett looked down at me.

'Well, Charlotte,' she said kindly. 'Did you write this note?'

There was a small scuffle at the back of the room and Angela stood up.

'I wrote it, Miss Bennett,' she confessed bravely, and I could have hugged her.

'We'll say no more about it, then,' said Miss Bennett, smiling at Angela warmly. 'Thank you for admitting it, Angela. You are a very truthful girl. But of course you must never do it again. And I'm afraid you must write the word "beautiful" three times in your green spelling book. I'm really quite surprised at you.'

'Yes, Miss Bennett. Thank you, Miss Bennett,' said Angela meekly, and sat down again. I was allowed to go back to my place and Angela threw me a huge smile when nobody was looking.

7

Miss Bennett collected all the compositions and began to glance through them while we put away our pencils and rubbers and tidied the classroom before going home. I saw her pick up one of the compositions to read out loud and I kept my fingers crossed hoping it was mine.

But it wasn't mine. It was that awful Delilah Jones's. And my stomach began to twitch as Miss Bennett read it. For I suddenly realized that of course Man's Best Friend was supposed to be a DOG!

Miss Bennett finished reading Delilah's boring old composition about dull old Saint Bernards rescuing stupid people off the tops of snow-covered mountains. Then she picked up another one and I squirmed in my seat as she peered at me over the top of her glasses.

'Somebody,' she said, 'SOMEbody didn't know that Man's Best Friend is a DOG! I find this very hard to believe, but SOMEbody wrote about a PERSON!'

My cheeks burned as everybody started to titter and giggle. But the worst was still to come.

'And not only that,' said Miss Bennett. 'SOMEbody can't even spell a simple word like "friend" without making a silly mistake.'

I hunched my shoulders and stared at the lid of my desk as Miss Bennett read out my first sentence. And I nearly died when I heard the terrible thing I had written.

'Angela Mitchell is my very best FIEND!'

Everybody laughed like mad. I hardly dared look at Angela, but when I did find the courage to peep over my shoulder I found that she was laughing harder than anybody. She didn't mind a bit.

Angela can always see the funny side of things. I think that's one of the reasons why I like her so much.

2

ONE wet morning during the Easter holidays Auntie Sally
was having coffee in the kitchen with my mum. Angela
and I were sitting on the floor doing a jigsaw puzzle on
a tray. We had sorted out all the pieces with straight
edges, because that's the best way to do a jigsaw puzzle.
You pick out all the straight edge bits first and do all the
outside like a frame. After that it's easy.

My mum and Auntie Sally were perched on stools at
opposite sides of the kitchen table drinking coffee out of
big brown mugs and eating shortbread biscuits. Auntie
Sally passed my mum the sugar and my mum said mercy
buckets, which is French for thank you, because she's
learning French at evening classes and she likes to show
off a bit. My dad laughed like anything when she told him
she was going to learn French, and said why couldn't she
learn something sensible and practical like needlework,

then maybe she'd do something about all those shirts hanging in the wardrobe that he couldn't wear because they had no buttons on. But my mum said she needed something intellectual and stimulating that would stretch her brain, and my dad laughed some more and said she should be careful she didn't stretch it too far, it might snap. That made her mad, and she started banging the dishes about in the sink. She got her own back, though. She signed him on for the gardening class.

Angela and I finished the frame of the jigsaw and she started picking out all the sky bits. I hate doing the sky bits. They all look the same and it's boring. I don't think the people who make jigsaw puzzles ever do them themselves. If they did they wouldn't make so many with all those sky bits.

'Did I ever tell you about the time we took Angela to a wedding when she was only three?' said Auntie Sally to my mum. 'She ate three whole platefuls of sherry trifle and then asked for more.'

'She obviously takes after her father,' said my mum, and they both snorted with laughter and Auntie Sally nearly choked in her coffee. I thought it was funny, too, so I laughed. But I realized I shouldn't have done when they both turned their heads and stared at me.

'What are you laughing at, Charlie?' asked my mum.

'I was laughing at what you said, Mum,' I explained. 'It was very funny, because Uncle Jim always . . .'

'That's quite enough, Charlie,' said my mum. 'You shouldn't have been listening. Off you go out to play. It's stopped raining now.'

Isn't it strange the way grown-ups expect you not to listen to their conversations even when they're in the same room with you. They must think you can switch off your ears or something. And have you noticed that it's always the most interesting bits that you're not supposed to hear, like when that pretty blonde Shirley Maddison from down the road ran away with the milk-man, or whether Mrs Scallicci from the fish and chip shop, who has six children already, is going to have another one, or about Mrs Todd in the next street who keeps seventeen cats and plays the trombone in a jazz band and never ever washes the kitchen floor. They never mind you listening to the boring things like what sort of cheese makes the best cheese soufflé or how many miles to the gallon Uncle Jim gets out of his new Morris Marina.

Angela and I put away the jigsaw puzzle and went ouside.

'Wellingtons,' said my mum, as we were just about to go out of the back door. 'And raincoats.' So we both had to come back in and change.

Outside it had stopped raining but everything was still wet and dripping.

'What shall we do?' said Angela, kicking moodily at a heap of old leaves with the toe of her boot. 'It's a hor-rible day.'

'Roller skates?' I suggested.

'Too wet,' said Angela.

'We could take Rover for a walk?' I said hopefully. Rover is my tortoise. I really wanted a dog but my mum won't let me have a dog because of hairs all over the house. So she bought me a tortoise instead and I called him Rover. My dad said it was a good idea to call him Rover, it does no harm to pretend. And Rover does like being taken for walks, although he doesn't seem to like his lead much.

'No,' said Angela. 'It would take too long. We have to go home in a few minutes because my mum has to bake a cake. That disgusting Miss Menzies is coming to tea this afternoon. You've got to come too, my mum said I could ask you.'

I made a face. Angela doesn't like Miss Menzies and neither do I. She must be the fattest lady in the world, and the greediest. My mum says maybe Miss Menzies can't help being fat, it could be her glands or something, but she's only being kind. Angela and I know that Miss Menzies is too fat simply because she eats too much. She's always inviting herself to tea and there's never anything left on the table when she's finished. I think she's even worse than Laurence Parker.

My mum feels sorry for Miss Menzies and said it must be awful to be that size and not to be able to buy dresses to fit you. My dad said that buying the dresses wasn't the problem, but taking off all the tent pegs and guy ropes when you got them home must be a bit of a nuisance. My mum said how could he say such a thing, and my dad laughed and said it was true. He said that Miss Menzies hung a blue dress on the line last week and squatters moved in. I didn't know what he meant, but I certainly didn't want to go to tea with her.

'Oh, Angela. Do I have to come?' I said. 'Last time she came to tea she ate all the sandwiches and we only had bread and butter.'

'Oh, please come, Charlie,' begged Angela, opening her blue eyes wide. 'It'll be awful without you. I won't be able to bear it.'

So of course I had to say yes.

We squelched down the garden to the playshed where we thought it might be a bit drier. The playshed is a small wooden hut that my dad built for us a long time ago and it's got a table and chairs and picnic things and a moth-eaten old fur rug on the floor, and there's a rocking horse and lots of dolls that we used to have tea parties with but we're both getting a bit too big for that now. We opened the door and it was all damp and dusty and gloomy inside.

'What a mess,' I said. 'Let's do a bit of spring cleaning.' And I took some dusters and a broom from the cupboard in the corner.

Angela didn't look at all keen on the idea so I started without her. She watched me flapping the duster about for a minute or two and then she must have decided it looked like fun after all, because she took the broom and began to sweep the cobwebs down from the ceiling.

We worked happily together for a while, raising clouds of dust and making ourselves sneeze. Then all at once Angela let out a horrible shriek and dropped the broom with a clatter as the biggest, blackest spider you ever saw tumbled down from the roof into the middle of the floor.

I loathe spiders. I particularly loathe fat round spiders with thick hairy legs like this one was. It was huge. We stared at it and shuddered but it just lay there and didn't move.

'Maybe it's dead,' said Angela, taking a step closer.

'It looks dead,' I agreed, and Angela began to prod it with the handle of the broom. 'Be careful,' I said. 'It might only be asleep. It might wake up and . . . and . . . scuttle at you!'

Angela poked it some more but the spider was definitely quite dead and wouldn't be scuttling at anybody any more. Angela put down the broom and began to hunt in the cupboard.

'What are you looking for?' I asked.

She looked at me with shining eyes. 'I'm looking for something to put it in,' she said. 'I'm going to take it home. I'm going to play a trick on Miss Menzies with it!'

'Oh!' I said, because I couldn't think of anything else to say. 'Oh, Angela!'

Just then we heard Angela's mum calling from the house.

'Angela! Come along, dear. Time to go.'

Angela scooped up the horrid spider into an empty tobacco tin and pressed the lid on it. She pushed it into the pocket of her raincoat.

''Bye, Charlie,' she said. 'See you later.' And she trotted away through the puddles to where her mum was waiting.

The afternoon started off badly because I wanted to wear my checked shirt and my cowboy jeans with the fringes down the sides and my mum insisted on me wearing my boring old navy blue dress with the white collar and cuffs and about a hundred buttons all down the front. And she made me scrub behind my ears and under my fingernails and wear clean white socks instead of the lovely purple and red stripey ones that Uncle Barrie had sent me for my birthday. She made me wear those awful black patent leather shoes that are too small for me and pinch my toes but she won't throw them away because they are still too new, and is it my fault if my feet are growing faster than my brain?

By half past three she was satisfied that I looked respectable enough and she let me go.

'And no walking in puddles!' she shouted after me as I went off down the drive, and she stood in the doorway and watched to make sure I didn't. But when I got round the corner into Angela's drive there was a huge muddy puddle right in front of me. So I jumped up and down in it a few times and splashed my legs and made my socks and shoes all wet and filthy. Auntie Sally opened the back door when I knocked and the first thing she noticed was my feet.

'Oh, Charlie!' she said. 'What happened to your shoes?'

'There's a great big puddle in your drive,' I said, as if that explained everything, and she clucked and tutted like anything and made me take my socks and shoes off in the kitchen and dry my legs and feet on a nice, warm, fluffy towel.

'I'll get you some of Angela's slippers to wear,' said Auntie Sally, and just then Angela came into the kitchen. She looked lovely. She was wearing a sort of cream-coloured dress with little brown flowers on it and a brown velvet ribbon in her hair to match the belt of the dress.

'Hello, Charlie,' she said and her eyes were all sparkly with excitement and mischief. There was a bulge in the pocket of her dress and she kept patting it and putting her finger to her lips in a stealthy sort of way. My stomach felt all funny as I remembered the spider and wondered what she was going to do with it.

Auntie Sally fetched me some slippers to wear and then left Angela and me alone in the kitchen.

'Come into the living room when you're ready, girls,' she said. 'Miss Menzies is already here.'

I finished drying my feet and put on Angela's slippers. They were pink satin with velvet bows on them and they made me feel like a dancer. I looked round to show Angela, but she was busy doing something at the kitchen table where all the food for the tea was laid out ready. I got up to have a look.

Angela had cut two small triangles from a slice of bread and butter and was struggling to take the lid off the tobacco tin.

'Angela!' I said, horrified. 'What are you doing?'

Angela grinned wickedly and did a little dance of glee from one foot to the other.

'Making a sandwich,' she said.

'Oh!' I said.

15

She managed to get the tin open and she shook the huge horrible hairy spider out on to one of the triangles of bread. I stared at it lying there on the yellow butter and I suddenly felt a bit sick. Angela picked up the other piece of bread and pressed it lightly down on top of the spider. Then she neatly trimmed off the crusts and put the sandwich on the plate on top of the others.

'Oh, Angela!' I breathed. 'You can't!'

'Why not?' said Angela carelessly, as she washed the knife and wiped away the crumbs. 'That'll teach the fat old faggot!'

'But Angela,' I said. 'How will you make sure that Miss Menzies gets the right one? It would be awful if . . .' And I gulped and swallowed hard.

'She's bound to,' said Angela. 'Because she's the guest. And you always offer the plate to the guest first.'

We went into the living room and there sat Miss Menzies in the biggest armchair which sagged in the middle under her weight. She was wearing a huge loose sort of kaftan thing of bright orange cotton with green swirly lines on it. Her hair was the same orange as her dress and she had rings of black stuff round her eyes like a panda. She had a pimple on her chin with a black bristle sticking out of it, and I couldn't help feeling sorry for her.

'And here come the darling little girls,' she cooed when Angela and I went in. 'Don't they look just ducky in their little dresses!'

We all made polite conversation for the next ten minutes or so. Angela chattered cheerfully about what we had been doing at school and how good her writing was and how Miss Bennett had given her a gold star for arithmetic. But I hardly said a word.

At last Auntie Sally brought in the teapot and announced that it was time for tea. Miss Menzies jumped up straight away and went to the table. Angela was sent to bring in the food from the kitchen and we all sat down. Then there was some more ghastly suspense because of course we had to eat bread and butter first.

You see, when you have a tea party you always have to eat things in a special order. First you eat two pieces of bread and butter and you're not allowed to say 'no thank you' but you must have them whether you want them or not. Then after the bread and butter you have the sandwiches, if you're lucky and the grown-ups haven't beaten you to it. After that you can have a piece of cake, and then last of all you are allowed to eat the chocolate biscuits. My mum says that it's called etiquette, but it seems a bit silly if you ask me. My Uncle Barrie, the one who sent me those lovely purple and red stripey socks for my birthday and who is an art teacher and plays the guitar and has hair almost as long as Angela's, says it doesn't matter in the least what order you eat things in. He says he often starts his dinner with apple pie or ice-cream and finishes with tomato soup.

'Do have a sandwich, Miss Menzies,' said Auntie Sally politely and my hands started to shake so much that I had to put my cup down quickly before I spilt my tea.

'Oh, thank you, how kind, I will if I may,' gushed Miss Menzies as Aunt Sally offered her the plate. She leaned forward and all six of her chins wobbled like mad. 'My, don't they look delicious!'

Angela winked at me and grinned as Miss Menzies' hand hovered over the sandwiches with her big fat fingers like pink sausages. But I couldn't bear it any longer. I did the only thing I could think of. I lurched forward in my chair and SNATCHED the top sandwich right from under Miss Menzies' nose and dropped it hurriedly on to my plate.

There was an astonished silence. Everybody stared at me. Angela made a little choking sound which could have been a smothered giggle. I knotted my hands in my lap and stared at the small sandwich on my plate. I could feel my face growing redder and redder.

'Well!' said Miss Menzies at last. 'What a very rude little girl!'

'I think Charlie must have left her manners at home today,' said Auntie Sally in a cross voice. 'I'm sorry, Miss Menzies. But never mind, there are plenty more sandwiches. Here, take one or two.'

Miss Menzies took four and I went on gazing miserably at my plate. I kept thinking about that nasty old spider lying in there with its fat black body and its thick hairy legs. I knew I couldn't eat that sandwich to save my life.

Auntie Sally noticed me sitting there doing nothing.

'Come along, Charlie,' she said. 'Eat up your sandwich. You were in a big enough hurry to get it, after all.'

'I don't think I feel very hungry, Auntie Sally,' I said in a small voice.

'Nonsense, child!' said Auntie Sally sharply. 'Eat up your sandwich at once or I'm afraid I shall have to send you home. I don't know what's come over you today, Charlie Ellis!'

If I hadn't known that it would make things worse I'd have gone home there and then. I wanted my dad. I knew he was home because our car had passed the window a few minutes before. I wanted to sit on my dad's knee and put my head on his shoulder and dip my finger in his glass of sherry which he lets me do when he's in a good mood.

And then my friend Angela did an extraordinary thing. She leaned over the table and picked up the sandwich from my plate.

'Charlie has just realised that the sandwiches are cucumber,' she explained. 'Charlie can't eat cucumber, you know. She's allergic to it.' She gave me a big smile.

18

'But don't worry, Charlie,' she said kindly. 'I'll eat it.' And she took a big bite out of the sandwich and munched it up as if it was caviar.

I couldn't believe my eyes. Angela ate the whole sandwich and then delicately licked the tips of her fingers.

'Delicious!' she said, patting her mouth daintily with her serviette. 'May I have some chocolate cake now, Mum?'

Somehow I managed to get through the rest of the meal and made myself swallow a small piece of cake and a biscuit. I kept looking at Angela anxiously, but she showed no ill effects whatever. I kept thinking what a noble and generous thing she had done, and what a wonderful friend she was, but I couldn't understand why she wasn't sick all over the table.

At last I managed to escape. I thanked Auntie Sally for my tea and apologized for my bad behaviour. She said not to worry, we all have our off days, and she was sorry about the sandwiches being cucumber. Angela went with me to the back door after I'd changed into my own socks and shoes which were now dry.

'Oh, Angela!' I whispered as she opened the door to let me out. 'I don't know how you did it, but you're the best friend in the whole world!'

Angela giggled. 'You should have seen your face!' she said. Then she took my hand and pulled me towards the pedal bin in the corner of the kitchen. She lifted the lid and pointed inside. I looked into the bin. There at the bottom lay a small white sandwich. I stared at it and then looked blankly into Angela's laughing face.

'That's the one with the spider in it,' she said. 'I didn't have the nerve to go through with it after all. I threw it in the bin when my mum sent me out to get the tea things.'

She opened the door for me and I stepped outside.

'Anyway,' she said innocently, before shutting the

door behind me. 'It would have been a very mean and unkind thing to do, wouldn't it?'

I went home, knowing quite well that Angela had played a trick on somebody that day. And it wasn't Miss Menzies at all. It was me.

3

I was lying on my bed one Saturday morning reading *The House At Pooh Corner* when Angela came round to see if I was coming out to play. I had just got to the bit where Tigger bounces Eeyore into the river, and I didn't want to stop reading at such an interesting place in the story, but I heard my mum telling Angela that I was upstairs in my room and to go straight up. So I shut the book and started to push it under the pillow before Angela could see it, but I wasn't quite quick enough and she caught me.

'Still reading that old rubbish, I see,' she said, marching into my room without knocking. I slid off the bed and put the book back on the shelf.

'It's not rubbish,' I said. 'My dad likes it too, so there!'

'Oh, your dad!' said Angela witheringly, as if to say everybody knows what a fool he is. 'Well, I think it's babyish. My cousin Dominic reads it, and he's only five and a half.'

'It's not babyish,' I said stoutly. 'My dad says it's packed with subtle humour. He says it's the second funniest book he's ever read.'

'What's the funniest?' asked Angela.

'Whinnie-The-Pooh,' I said, and Angela made a disgusted face.

'I don't know why you want to lie around indoors reading on a nice day like this, anyway,' she said, waving a hand towards the window. I looked outside and saw that she was right, it really was a lovely morning. The sky was blue and the sparrows in the tree outside my window were cheeping like mad in the sunshine.

'What do you want to do?' I said.

'I thought we'd go and pick bluebells,' said Angela. 'I promised Miss Bennett I'd try to get some for her. She wants to decorate the school hall for the PTA meeting this afternoon.'

A PTA meeting is when all the mums and dads have to go to school to see our work and talk to the teachers and we're never allowed to go because they all want to talk about us behind our backs. My dad moans and groans like anything when they have a PTA meeting on a Saturday afternoon because it interferes with his football on the telly and my mum says what sort of a father is he to put Newcastle United before the welfare of his only child. Miss Bennett always makes us tidy our desks on the Friday before, and the classroom is all spick and span and shining and full of flowers and everybody pretends it's like that all the time and the teachers even get their hair done. So I thought it was a good idea to get some bluebells for Miss Bennett.

'Yes, all right,' I said to Angela. 'Let's do that. It'll be nice in the woods.'

When my mum heard we were going to the woods she made me wear my wellingtons and my old green anorak with the torn lining, even though Angela was wearing that new pink denim trouser suit of hers with the white stitching all round the pockets. My mum even made me put on my woolly bobble-hat and scarf because I was just getting better from that cold I caught when Angela and I fell in the river, and she didn't want me catching pneumonia.

'And you're not to go any further than Lane End Beeches,' said my mum as we were leaving. 'I want you back at a reasonable time for lunch.'

To get to Lane End Beeches you have to walk right through the village and across the bridge over the Thames and then follow the main road for about a mile. Then there's a lane on the left which leads into a sort of picnic area with a car park and a patch of woodland, but it's not really all that nice. It's full of old car tyres and sweet papers and empty coke tins and cigarette packets because a lot of people go there and never pick up their rubbish, and my dad says it's a shame we don't get the Wombles this far out.

But when we reached the turning for Lane End Beeches Angela walked straight on. I had to stop and shout at her.

'Hey!' I called. 'We're here. It's this way.'

Angela shook her head and hurried on. I ran after her and caught her up.

'Where are you going?' I said breathlessly. 'We've passed the way in to Lane End Beeches.'

Angela tossed her head. 'Oh, we're not going there,' she said. 'Everybody goes there. It's all mucky and full of rubbish and all the bluebells have either been picked or trampled on ages ago.'

'But where are we going, then?' I said anxiously. I hoped she wasn't going to say Jason's Wood because that's private land and belongs to a very rich man who's a lord or something and hardly anybody in the village even knows what he looks like because he never comes out from behind his eight foot high iron gates.

'We're going to Jason's Wood,' said Angela. 'There'll be lots of bluebells there.'

'Oh!' I said. I didn't argue. She had that look on her face. The one that means arguing won't do the slightest bit of good.

We crossed the main road and began to follow a track off to the right. We walked along beside a high brick wall with bits of broken glass stuck in the cement at the top. There were notices on the wall every so often which said 'Private Property' and 'Keep Out' and 'No Trespassing'. After a while the wall ended and became a wooden fence, but there was barbed wire along the top and I couldn't help feeling relieved. Even Angela wouldn't be able to get in there.

I was wrong. She stopped suddenly and said 'Ah! Here we are. Just what we need.' I stopped too and looked. Growing close against the fence was an old tree, all lumpy and gnarled and covered with ivy and creepers. One of its branches leaned over the top of the fence and reached into the woods beyond. A large wooden sign on the fence said 'Trespassers Will Be Prosecuted.'

'We'll climb up the tree, wriggle along that branch and then jump down,' said Angela. 'Easy!'

'Oh, Angela, I don't think we should,' I said.

She planted her feet apart and put her hands on her hips.

'Charlie Ellis!' she said. 'You're scared!'

'Scared?' I said. 'Who me?' I said. 'Of course not!'

So we climbed the tree and Angela was right, it was easy, except I caught the lining of my anorak on a branch and ripped it a bit more. We dropped down from the branch and were soon standing in a little grassy clearing just inside the fence.

Everything was quiet and peaceful. The sunlight shone down through the trees and made big pools of gold among the grass and fern. Somewhere above our heads a bird sang a lovely trickly song.

'Angela,' I whispered. 'What does "prosecuted" mean?'

Angela thought for a minute. 'Well,' she said, 'I think it's like a sort of electric chair. They strap you in a seat made of some kind of metal, and fix wires to you, and then they press a switch that sends an electric shock right through your body. I forget how many volts it is,' she added carelessly. 'About a million, I think.'

'And does it kill you?' I asked, a bit shakily.

'Oh, yes, of course,' said Angela airily. 'They still use it to kill murderers in some countries. Quite clever really. It probably doesn't even hurt.'

I didn't think it was clever at all. And I bet it hurt like mad. Anyway, nobody could be cruel enough to do that to people for just trespassing in a wood. I was just about to tell Angela so when I suddenly saw thousands of bluebells, all spread out in front of us like a thick blue carpet. Angela spotted them at the same time and ran forward with a cry of delight.

They were the nicest bluebells I had ever seen. They were the deepest blue you can imagine, with long stalks and that lovely cool smell. Before long I had gathered a great armful, so I stopped picking for a moment and looked round for Angela. But I must have wandered a long way without noticing for there was no sign of her at all. I was quite alone.

25

The wood was all sort of silent and still and I stood there for a long time just smelling the flowers in my arms and looking around at all the different shades of green. Suddenly there was a soft rustle in the ferns beside me and something happened that made me hold my breath and stare. A whole family of pheasants stepped out of the shadows into a patch of sunlight right by my feet.

I knew they were pheasants because I've seen pictures of them in books and I've seen dead ones hanging upside down in the butcher's shop. But I'd never seen real live ones before, and I was so thrilled I could hardly breathe. They didn't seem a bit afraid of me, and I stood as still as a statue and watched them. The father was much prettier than the mother, and he had lovely golden feathers on his neck and a long pointed tail that bobbed up and down when he walked. Have you noticed that with birds it's always the fathers who dress up in the brightest colours and the mothers all wear boring old greys and browns? I bet my mum's glad she isn't a bird.

But best of all were the babies. I counted them and there were sixteen. Sixteen little stripey balls of fluff about the size of a ping-pong ball. They scratched about and pecked among the leaves and I couldn't take my eyes off them. I only wished Angela was here to see them too.

I don't know how long I stood there just looking at them, but suddenly I got the fright of my life when I heard a twig snap loudly right behind me. A heavy hand came down on my shoulder and a man's deep voice said,

'And what are you up to, young lady?'

Honestly, I nearly jumped out of my skin. I turned round quickly and there was this huge tall man with black hair and a beard. He had a tweedy sort of jacket on and thick brown corduroy trousers and wellingtons.

He had a great big gun resting on his shoulder, and I stared at it and said nothing.

The man looked at me and at my big bundle of bluebells. He shook his head sternly.

'Trespassing, eh?' he said. 'Stealing flowers, eh?' He nodded towards the pheasants still picking at the leaves. 'Disturbing the GAME, eh?'

When I still didn't say anything he shook his head again and shifted his gun to the other shoulder.

'I think you'd better come along with me,' he said. 'Sir Edmund will want to have a word with you.' And he turned his back on me and began to walk away through the trees, expecting me to follow.

I thought of running away, but I knew it wouldn't do any good. I suddenly had this terrible picture in my mind of me stumbling wildly through the woods with shots echoing round my ears and bullets bouncing off the trees, and I saw myself tumbling down in a heap among the leaves with blood pouring out of a big hole in my back, and my mum's white face when I was carried home on a stretcher with a blanket over my face, and I knew I shouldn't have watched that horrible film on the telly last night.

Anyway I took a deep breath and started to trail along towards the keeper, who had turned round and was waiting for me to catch up. I think he must have felt sorry for me, because he started to chat quite kindly to me as we went along. He said he would have let me go, only he didn't like to risk losing his job. Sir Edmund had been getting very mad recently with people tramping about in his wood, and he had told the keeper that he wanted to deal with the next one personally.

'In fact,' said the keeper regretfully. 'It wouldn't surprise me if he actually decided to prosecute this time. Just to set an example, like, you know.'

'Do . . . do you really think so?' I said faintly.

'Well, I don't like to worry you,' said the keeper. 'But I reckon it's more than likely.'

Well of course I wasn't stupid enough to believe all that rubbish Angela had told me about metal chairs and electric wires and things, but all the same I couldn't help feeling a bit worried about what sort of horrible things were going to happen to me when I got prosecuted. So I wasn't very happy as I followed the keeper out of the wood and down a long gravel drive towards Sir Edmund Jason's big white house.

We went into the house through a door at the side and the keeper spoke to a maid in a black dress and a frilly white apron. She stared at me so hard that I felt like putting my tongue out at her, but I didn't quite dare, even though I knew she was turning her nose up at my tatty anorak and my old woolly hat and muddy wellies. She told the keeper that Sir Edmund was in his study and we walked down a long passage with a green carpet and dusty old pictures of ladies and gentlemen in funny clothes with a few dogs that didn't look like dogs at all but looked more like sheep. Have you noticed that dogs in old-fashioned paintings nearly always look like sheep? Perhaps they're meant to be sheepdogs.

We crossed a big sort of hall place with a polished floor and coloured rugs and plants in pots and flowers everywhere and a strong smell of cigar smoke and lavender wax polish. The keeper knocked at a door and a growly voice told us to come. Not come in. Just come.

The keeper propped his gun carefully against the wall. Then he opened the door and gently pushed me forward into the room in front of him.

'Found this one in the woods picking bluebells, Sir Edmund,' he explained, and I realized that I was still clutching them in my arms.

A short, fat man got up from behind a polished wooden desk and came towards us. He made a tut-tutting noise and looked cross.

'Thank you, Parkinson,' he said. 'You did quite right to bring her to me.'

I had a good look at Sir Edmund Jason. He's sort of small and round with a big head as bald as Kojak's, but you can tell straightaway that he's a lord because of his nose. I read in a book once that all lords and ladies have blue blood and if that's true then Sir Edmund Jason must be a very high-up lord indeed because he's got this great hooked nose and you can actually see the blue veins in it. He's got the bluest nose I've ever seen. It's so blue it's almost purple.

Anyway, I stared at him and he stared at me and his eyebrows twitched a bit, and then he began to pace up and down on the rug in front of his desk. Mr Parkinson stood with his back to the door like a sentry.

'It's quite intolerable,' said Sir Edmund at last. 'I've done everything I can. Broken glass on the walls. Barbed wire on the fences. Plenty of warning notices. Two full-time keepers. And still the bally poachers and marauding kids get in. It's time I put a stop to it once and for all. I've been far too lenient in the past.' He stopped pacing and turned to face me. 'Young lady,' he said severely, 'I'm afraid I shall have to prosecute you.'

My knees shook a bit as Sir Edmund sat down again behind his desk and took out a sheet of paper and a pen.

'Now then,' he said. 'You'd better tell me your name and address.'

I couldn't speak. I think I gave a sort of croak. Sir Edmund looked at me over the desk and I could tell that he was beginning to feel sorry for me.

'I've got to think of my birds, you know,' he said, quite kindly. 'After all, it is the breeding season.'

And then he started telling me all about his pheasants, and in spite of the trouble I was in I couldn't help being interested. He told me all about their nests in the ferns, and about the dreadful damage people do when they trample about in the woods. 'They tread on the eggs and terrify the mothers, and chicks are often abandoned if the nest is disturbed. As if we didn't have enough trouble saving them from the foxes and rats and weasels and crows and such like. So you see, I must do everything I can to protect them.'

I thought about those lovely birds I had seen in the wood and I knew he was right. I thought he must be a nice man to care so much for wildlife. My dad always says that the best people are the ones who care about animals.

'Yes, I see,' I said in a small voice. 'You must have an awful lot of pheasants.'

'Oh, a tremendous number,' said Sir Edmund. 'This is one of the best game woods in the whole of England. All my friends come down from London. Even Royalty. Terrific parties we have, you know, in the shooting season.'

'Shooting?' I said. 'Shooting what?'

'Why, the pheasants, of course!' he said, getting all excited. 'That's what they're FOR, dammit! Out with a dog and a gun on a splendid crisp December morning, and all that. Bang, bang! Terrific fun, you know.'

I still couldn't believe it. 'You mean you kill them?' I said. 'What for? For food?'

'No, no, of course not,' said Sir Edmund impatiently. 'Although we do eat a few of them afterwards and jolly tasty they are too with a nice drop of claret. No, no, my dear young lady. The whole point of it all is the fun of it. It's SPORT!'

I stared at him for a minute. And then I got mad. I

was just about as mad as Angela was that time at school when Miss Bennett chose me instead of her to be the prince in the Christmas play. I forgot all about being prosecuted and I started telling that Sir Edmund Jason just exactly what I thought of him. I yelled and stamped and flung his rotten old bluebells in a heap on the floor.

'Those poor little birds,' I shouted. 'To be kept in that wood ... and guarded ... and protected ... and fed and looked after ... only until they are big enough for you and your friends to go out and SHOOT!' I took a deep breath. 'I think you're mean and nasty and horrible,' I said. 'Even if you have got a blue nose!'

I stood there glaring while Sir Edmund just sat and blinked with his mouth open. Mr Parkinson shuffled his feet and looked a bit uncomfortable. Suddenly there was a tap at the door.

'Come,' said Sir Edmund weakly. The door opened a few inches and the maid stuck her head round the edge.

'Sorry to interrupt, Sir Edmund,' she said. 'But there's a little girl here who insists on seeing you, and I thought it might be something to do with ...'

The maid didn't have time to finish what she was saying. She was rudely pushed aside and who should come marching into the room but my friend Angela. She looked as defiant as anything with her cheeks all pink and her hair all wild and tumbled and full of leaves and bits of twig. Her trouser suit was filthy and there were green stains all round the knees. She came straight to where I was standing and put her arms round me.

'I've come to save my friend from getting prosecuted,' she declared stoutly.

I felt like cheering the way my dad and I do when we're watching a cowboy film on the telly and John Wayne's girlfriend is just about to be scalped by the

Indians when the cavalry suddenly comes galloping over the hill to the rescue. Sir Edmund looked at Angela and his mouth opened and shut a few times like a goldfish and his nose seemed to be going bluer than ever.

'Well,' he said. 'Well, well, well.' Isn't it awful the way grown-ups keep on saying 'well'? Angela and I once counted how many times the vicar said well during a sermon and we made it a hundred and twelve.

'Well,' said Sir Edmund again. 'I'm afraid I've already made up my mind to take proceedings.'

'Please don't, Sir Edmund,' wailed Angela, starting to wring her hands together the way my mum does when the yorkshire puddings won't rise and my dad's boss is coming to dinner. Then she went into action and did her tragedy queen act right in the middle of Sir Edmund's rug.

I bet you've never seen anything like Angela's tragedy queen act. My dad says she makes Lady Macbeth look like something out of the Muppet Show. I didn't bat an eyelid because I've seen it all before, like that time in the shoe shop in Oxford Street when Auntie Sally wouldn't buy her those red leather shoes with the black bows. But it fooled Sir Edmund completely.

He rushed out from behind his desk and lifted Angela into a big armchair. He patted her hands and stroked her hair and made there-there noises and looked helplessly at Mr Parkinson and the maid who only looked at one another and did nothing and I could see that they weren't fooled either. At last Angela calmed down a bit and pushed her hair out of her eyes.

'Don't prosecute my friend,' she said to Sir Edmund with a sort of sob in her voice. 'It was all my fault we were in the woods. Prosecute me instead.'

'It's all right,' said Sir Edmund hastily. 'Nobody is going to prosecute anybody. You can both go home, and the sooner the better.' He took a large silk hanky out of his pocket and mopped his face.

'Get rid of them, Parkinson,' he said faintly to the keeper. Then he turned to the maid. 'I want a very large brandy and soda immediately, Marie,' he said. 'And please fetch me one of my yellow pills.'

Mr Parkinson opened the door and we began to troop out into the hall, but suddenly Angela darted back into the room and scooped up the heap of bluebells from the floor.

'Oops, nearly forgot them,' she said to Sir Edmund with one of her most dazzling smiles.

When Mr Parkinson let Angela and me out of the big iron gates we found ourselves back on the main road again not far from the village. We set off home at a trot in case we were late for lunch.

'At least we've still got my bluebells,' I said, as we drew near the school. 'We might as well pop in and give them to Miss Bennett.'

'Yes,' said Angela. 'But I think I should be the one to give them to her, don't you? It was only because of having to rescue you that I had to leave mine in the woods. I hope you realize that I had to crawl absolutely miles on my hands and knees following you and that keeper. And I did save you from getting prosecuted, didn't I?'

And of course I had to agree.

However, when I asked my dad about it later, he told me that being prosecuted isn't a bit like what Angela said it was. He said all that happens is you have to go to a sort of courtroom place where some stern people sit on a bench and talk about what a bad girl you are and a kind lady tells you off and makes you promise not to do it again. And that's all there is to it.

And I bet Angela knew all the time what it really meant. She really is rotten to me sometimes.

4

FRIDAYS are special days at our school because instead of having Junior Prayers separately like we usually do, the whole school has Assembly together in the big hall and Miss Collingwood takes us. Miss Collingwood is the headmistress and I think she's lovely. She's tall and dark-haired and pretty and she's got a nice gentle voice and a kind smile. Nobody has ever seen her get mad or heard her shout and somehow she never seems to need to, because everybody always does what she wants anyway. And she never orders people about, she always asks them nicely. Not like my bossy Miss Bennett.

I like going to Assembly with the Upper School. The teachers sit on a row of chairs on the platform, and it's just like a stage and you can have a good look at them all. We have to stand in front of them and stare straight at their legs and feet, and you can't help noticing if any of the lady teachers have got holes in their tights and what colour socks the men teachers are wearing and whether they have polished their shoes.

First of all we have to sing a hymn together and Angela and I like to watch to see which teachers are really singing properly and which ones are just yawning or looking out of the window. And Mr Young, the music teacher, thumps away like anything on the piano and plays a lot of twiddly bits between the verses and Angela thinks he's even better than Elton John. Then we say our prayers and one of the big boys or girls from the top class reads the Lesson only I don't know why it's called the Lesson because it's just a bit out of the Bible and you don't really learn anything much. And sometimes it's Roger Grant's turn to read the Lesson, and then all the girls stare at him because he's the head boy and he's thirteen and he's got shiny brown hair and white teeth and looks exactly like Donny Osmond and everybody wants to marry him except Angela who has made up her mind to marry a king.

After the Lesson we all sing another hymn and then Miss Collingwood gives us one of her little chats. She calls it a chat but it's not really because she's the only one who's allowed to talk and we all have to stand still and not fidget. Miss Collingwood's little chats are about all sorts of things, like Cleanliness, and Truthfulness, and Helping Others, and stuff like that, and somehow she always makes you end up feeling ashamed of yourself for not being as clean or as honest or as helpful as you should be, and you secretly make up your mind to try harder in the future.

One Friday morning Miss Collingwood's little chat was

about Bad Language. Some boys at the back of the hall started to snigger when she said that, but they soon stopped when she gave them one of her looks. She told us that one of the Upper School boys, who really ought to know better, had been heard saying a very rude word on a bus. Miss Collingwood didn't tell us what the rude word was which was a shame because I was dying to know. But it must have been something very bad indeed because a lady on the bus was so shocked that she told the conductor, and the conductor took the boy's name and reported him to the school.

Miss Collingwood was very upset. She said it was a terrible thing for young people to swear and it damaged the school's good reputation and what a pity it was that so many of us were getting into this bad habit. She was determined not to let it happen in her school. She gazed down at us earnestly and we all turned our faces up towards her like rows of flowers looking at the sun. You felt as if she could see inside you and read what you were thinking and it was a very uncomfortable feeling.

'I'm going to ask you all to help me,' she said. 'Because there's only one way to stamp this out before it spreads. Now, you all know how much I dislike people telling tales, but I feel that in this important matter your loyalty to the school, and to me, should come before your loyalty to your friends. So, if any of you hear any person in this school using bad language I want you to tell one of the teachers at once, and the teacher will send that person to me. I know it's unpleasant, but I believe that in this case it's necessary. I'm sure I can rely on your support.'

Miss Collingwood gave us one of her nicest smiles and then nodded at Mr Young who was still sitting at the piano. He began to play his favourite marching tune and I think it's called Spaghetti March or something like that, and we all filed out with a lot of whispering and giggling

36

and everybody wondering who would be the first to get reported and feeling sure it wouldn't be them.

When we got back to the classroom it was time for our History lesson. I usually like History lessons, but this particular morning I couldn't seem to concentrate very well because I had a letter from my Uncle Barrie in my satchel. It had arrived just as I was leaving the house and I hadn't had time to open it yet. Uncle Barrie writes to me a lot and I love getting his letters because they're long and chatty and he puts funny poems in and sometimes there's even a postal order. So I kept thinking about it and dying for playtime so that I could open it and I didn't take much notice of the History lesson at all.

The lesson was about Captain Cook's voyages and the old-fashioned sailing ships and how the sailors kept on dying of a horrible disease called scurvy. And it was all because nobody had discovered that the disease could be prevented as easily as anything by eating fresh fruit and green vegetables that have something called Vitamin C in them. And then this Captain Cook found out that if he made all his sailors eat lemons and limes then nobody on his ship got scurvy and the Navy were so pleased that they gave him a medal. At the end of the lesson Miss Bennett started to ask us some questions about it and it was just my rotten luck that she picked on me first.

'Charlotte,' she said. 'Will you please tell us what happens to people who don't eat green vegetables.'

And without thinking I stood up and said the first thing that came into my head.

'They don't get any pudding,' I said, and gazed round the room in surprise as everybody burst out laughing. That fat Laurence Parker almost choked and even Miss Bennett's mouth twitched in a funny way and I thought she was going to laugh, too. She didn't, though. She got cross instead.

'Charlotte Ellis!' she snapped. 'You haven't listened to a single word of this lesson. You will stay indoors at break time and read the chapter on Captain Cook in your history book.'

'Yes, Miss Bennett,' I said, and tried to look sorry. But I didn't mind a bit really, because it would give me a chance to read my letter from Uncle Barrie in peace.

So when the bell went at playtime and everybody else went out into the playground with their apples and biscuits and Miss Bennett went off to the staffroom to have her coffee, I stayed in the classroom all by myself and read about Captain Cook. And it was very interesting, much more interesting than when Miss Bennett told it. She's the sort of person who could make even Doctor Who sound boring.

When I'd read the whole chapter I opened my letter from Uncle Barrie and it was lovely, all about the wild kids in his school in London and about the plays and films he had been to see and there was a postal order for fifty pence and a funny poem that made me giggle.

"There was a young sailor called Plum,
Who drank a whole barrel of rum,
He made himself drunk
And fell off his bunk
And landed flat on his elbow.'

I was just putting the letter away in my satchel when Miss Bennett came back into the classroom.

'Well, Charlotte,' she said. 'Have you read all about Captain Cook?'

'Yes, Miss Bennett,' I said meekly.

'And now do you know what happens to people who don't eat green vegetables?'

'Yes, Miss Bennett,' I said. 'They get scurvy.'

'Very well, Charlotte,' said Miss Bennett. 'You may go out for the last five minutes of break time. And please see that you pay more attention in future.'

'Yes, Miss Bennett. Thank you, Miss Bennett,' I said gratefully. Then I ran out of the room and down the corridor before she could change her mind. So that was how I got to the playground just in time to see Angela's accident.

They were all playing 'What's The Time Mr Wolf?' and Laurence Parker was the wolf. It may seem a bit of a silly game to play, but if you have to spend your playtime in a sort of concrete cage with iron railings round it there's not much else you can do except play silly games. Anyway, everybody was marching along behind Laurence Parker shouting 'What's the TIME, Mr Wolf?' and he kept saying it was five o'clock or seven o'clock or half past eleven and then suddenly he shouted 'DINNER TIME!' and everybody screamed and ran away and Laurence Parker started to chase Angela. I don't know why it is that whenever there's a chasing game going on it's always Angela who gets chased but that's what always happens.

So of course Angela shrieked and dashed away across the playground and that's when that awful Delilah Jones deliberately stuck her foot out in front of Angela and sent her crashing forward onto her knees.

Everybody crowded round and I had to elbow my way to the front to see what was happening. Angela was sitting on the ground holding her left leg which had blood pouring from a great gash in the knee. I noticed that she was keeping her leg bent sideways so that the blood dripped on the ground because she had her new white lace knee-socks on and she didn't want to get them stained. I knelt beside her and pushed her sock down towards her ankle away from the trickles of blood. She looked a bit pale but apart from that she seemed all right and I sent that nice David Watkins to find the teacher on duty. It's funny that teachers on duty never seem to be around when they're needed and yet they always manage to turn up when you least want them to.

Well, we were all standing around waiting for the teacher when that fat fool Laurence Parker started pulling Angela's arm and trying to make her stand up. I could see she didn't want to in case she got blood on her sock so I pushed him out of the way.

'Leave her alone, stupid!' I said. 'Can't you see she can't move her bloody leg!'

There was a shocked silence and then everybody started to gasp and say 'Ooh!' Delilah Jones put her hand to her mouth and her eyes went wide.

'Ooh, Charlie Ellis!' she said. 'You SWORE!'

Now what I don't understand is why a perfectly good and useful word like bloody should be a swear word. What else can you call something when it's all covered in blood except bloody? I think it's only a swear word because grown-ups have turned it into one and it's all their fault. And anyway they use it all the time. I even heard my dad say it once when he couldn't find a single pair of socks without holes in them.

'What rubbish!' I said. 'That wasn't swearing. I only said her leg was bloody because it is! Look at it,' I said. 'You can see it's bloody!'

Everybody started talking at once and I could feel my face getting more and more red. 'She said it again!' they said, and 'Ooh, did you hear that!' and 'Ooh, what language!' and they all pretended to be terribly shocked and before long there was a great crowd around us all having a lovely time saying wasn't Charlie Ellis wicked and not one of them taking the slightest bit of notice of Angela sitting on the ground bleeding to death.

Suddenly everybody went quiet as the teacher on duty arrived and my heart sank because it was Mrs Mason. Mrs Mason is the Scripture teacher and she's horrible. She's always talking about love and forgiveness and she's got a worse temper than anybody I know. I once saw her shaking a poor little kindergarten boy until his teeth nearly fell out because he accidentally put his sticky hands on her skirt.

'Whatever's going on here?' she said, and then she noticed Angela sitting on the ground. 'Oh, my goodness!' she said. 'You have had a nasty tumble.' She knelt at Angela's side and mopped up the worst of the blood with a wad of paper tissues that she had in her pocket. Then she tied a big white handkerchief around Angela's knee. When she'd finished she stood up and looked at us.

'Now,' she said. 'What was all that fuss about?'

Delilah Jones stepped forward. 'Please, Mrs Mason,' she said. 'Charlie Ellis said a bad word.'

Mrs Mason frowned at me. 'Charlie, is this true?' she said.

I shook my head and started to explain but everybody else nodded like mad and said they'd all heard me so what could I do?

'And what was this bad word?' Mrs Mason asked Delilah Jones, but Delilah put her hand over her mouth and went pink and tittered and said she couldn't say it, she just couldn't.

'Well, somebody had better tell me,' said Mrs Mason crossly. 'Miss Collingwood will certainly want to know.' But they all just looked at one another and looked at the ground and nobody said anything because nobody wanted to be the one to say that dreadful word.

'Well, actually, Mrs Mason,' said Delilah Jones at last, and she blushed and stammered like anything. 'Actually, er, Charlie said, er, bloody.'

41

Mrs Mason looked at Angela. 'Is this true, Angela? I'm sure I can rely on you to tell the truth.'

Angela gazed at Mrs Mason with her eyes all round and blue and innocent, and I knew there was no hope.

'Yes, Mrs Mason,' she said. 'She said it three times.'

I was very upset. 'It's not fair!' I shouted. 'I wasn't swearing at all! I only said that her leg was . . .'

'Charlotte!' snapped Mrs Mason. 'That will be quite enough. You'll only make things worse by trying to tell lies about it. You will go straight to Miss Collingwood's study at once. And you will tell her exactly why I have sent you.'

Everybody watched in silence as I began to trail miserably across the playground to the school. I looked back before I went in and saw that two of the bigger boys had linked hands to make a sort of chair and were carrying Angela back to the classroom. She gave me a wave to show that we were still friends but I didn't wave back. Somehow I just didn't feel like it. I stumped along the corridor to Miss Collingwood's room and knocked on the door so softly you could hardly hear it. Nothing happened so I sat down on the green chair to wait.

The green chair is a wooden seat and it's hard and uncomfortable and painted green and it stays outside Miss Collingwood's room for people who have done bad things to sit on while they wait for Miss Collingwood to see them. And it's awful because you're not allowed to go straight in but you have to knock and then wait until she comes out and sometimes you have to wait ages because she's busy seeing parents and sometimes she's not even there but taking a class somewhere and you might have to sit there for hours. And everybody who walks past knows what you're sitting there for and they shake their heads and go tut-tut and say what a naughty girl you are, and you get more and more ashamed and embarrassed.

But this time I didn't have long to wait. After only a minute or so the door opened and there stood Miss Collingwood, smiling.

'Come in, Charlie,' she said. 'What can I do for you?'

And do you know, I felt so miserable and upset and helpless and sorry for myself that I started to cry. Big tears rolled down my face and I rubbed my eyes and gulped and hiccupped.

'Dear me,' said Miss Collingwood kindly. 'We are in a state.'

I don't know why she said that WE were in a state when it was only me that was in one, but I was glad when she pushed a box of tissues in my hand because crying always gives me a runny nose. She made me sit down in a chair beside her desk and started looking at some papers to give me time to pull myself together.

I blew my nose and mopped up the tears and sniffed a bit. After that I found I was feeling much better. And you won't believe it but when I explained the whole thing to Miss Collingwood she understood perfectly. She said she felt exactly the same as me about it. She said what a shame it was that people misused the English language and spoiled it for everybody else, and that I hadn't used a bad word at all, it was all a question of context, whatever that means, and I wasn't to worry about it any more. And she patted my hand and gave me one of those posh chocolate peppermint creams in the little square brown envelopes that people have at dinner parties and promised to explain everything to Mrs Mason. Then she sent me back to the classroom.

When everybody saw my red eyes they thought I must have been in terrible trouble and they were all very nice to me for the rest of that day. I think they were all a bit ashamed of themselves for telling on me because even Laurence Parker gave me one of his toffees.

And of course I was furious with Angela. I even vowed

to myself that I would never be friends with her again. But I can never stay cross with her for long, and when it was home time and she hobbled out of school like a wounded hero with a great big sticking plaster on her knee, somehow I couldn't help forgiving her, especially when she wouldn't lean on anybody else's arm but mine.

5

THE day Angela and I fell in the river started out as one of those bright sunny mornings when spring tries to pretend that it's summer. It was a Sunday, and the phone rang quite early when I was still in bed and my dad shouted up the stairs that it was for me. I didn't really want to get up because I like to have a long lie-in on Sunday mornings and anyway I was all warm and snug and comfy cuddling Benjamin. Benjamin is my teddy bear and he's exactly the same age as me which is extremely old for a teddy bear, and he's a bit worn and tatty and one ear is missing but he's still lovely to cuddle. If Angela ever found out that I still take Benjamin to bed she'd laugh like anything because she gave all her teddies and things to the jumble sale ages ago. But my dad says you shouldn't abandon a faithful companion just because he's getting old and tatty and he's right. And my mum says it's lucky for him that she thinks so, too.

My mum was still in bed as well, but my dad always gets up early on Sunday mornings because he likes to read the Sunday papers in peace. As soon as my mum gets up she starts telling him to mow the lawn or mend the washing machine or put up a new shelf in the kitchen so it's the only chance he gets.

'It's Angela,' he said, when I stuck my head over the banister. I padded downstairs to the hall in my nightie and bare feet, blinking and yawning in the bright sunshine that poured in through the window and made a nice warm patch on our red carpet.

'Hello,' I said sleepily, picking up the phone.

'Hello,' said a strange croaky voice. 'Guess who this is.'

'Rod Stewart?' I said.

'Wrong,' said the voice.

'Donald Duck?' I said.

'Wrong again,' said the voice, giggling.

'I know,' I said. 'It's Angela.'

'Right,' said Angela, in her normal voice. 'You have just won a holiday for two at Clapham Junction.'

'What's the matter?' I said, yawning some more. 'You're up early.'

'I hope I got you out of bed,' said Angela, and she sounded all pleased and excited. 'Because it's a lovely sunny day and I've had a great idea. We're going on a ten mile walk.'

'Who is?' I said stupidly. 'What are you talking about?'

'A walk, dopey!' said Angela. 'A nice long one. Just you and me. We'll take heaps of sandwiches and things and have a picnic. We'll go all the way up the Thames

46

to Barlow and come back down the other side. My dad says it's ten miles at least and probably nearer twelve.'

'Oh,' I said. 'It sounds like an awful long way.'

'It is a long way, stupid,' said Angela. 'That's the whole point. It makes it worth going. Like a sort of expedition.'

'Oh, I said. 'Yes. I suppose so.'

'Well, you sound dead enthusiastic, I must say,' said Angela huffily. 'If you don't want to go just say so. I can always ask Delilah Jones.'

'Don't be silly, of course I want to go,' I said. 'But I'll have to ask my mum and ring you back.'

I was half hoping that my mum would say no, but when I went into her room to ask her she said it sounded like a very good idea.

'The fresh air and the exercise will do you the world of good,' she said. 'I'll get up in a second and make you some sandwiches.'

Angela was as pleased as anything when I rang her back and told her that it was all right for me to go.

'I'll be round in half an hour,' she said. 'My mum's packing my lunch now. I'm bringing salmon sandwiches and a leg of cold chicken and some chocolate biscuits. What are you bringing?'

'Pâté de foie,' I said recklessly, knowing quite well it would be Marmite or peanut butter.

'Coo!' said Angela. 'You lucky thing!'

I put the phone down and went upstairs to get washed and dressed. I looked in my wardrobe and decided to wear my white polo-necked jumper and my blue jeans and my red sandals.

'Very nice, too,' said my dad over the top of his newspaper when I came downstairs again. 'Red, white and blue. Most patriotic.' And he started to whistle 'Rule Britannia.'

My mum was in the kitchen in her dressing gown

making sandwiches and there was a boiled egg and some toast ready on the kitchen table for my breakfast. I had a look at the sandwiches and they were peanut butter.

'Oh, Mum,' I said. 'Do I have to have peanut butter? Angela's bringing salmon sandwiches and chicken leg and chocolate biscuits.'

'There's nothing wrong with peanut butter,' said my mum. 'It's every bit as nourishing as salmon or chicken. Probably more so. You can have some Marmite ones as well, if you like.'

I knew it was no use arguing so I started to eat my egg while my mum put the sandwiches and a piece of home-made ginger cake and two tins of coke into my blue canvas bag with the shoulder-strap. Then Angela arrived wearing brown dungarees and a brown and yellow striped jumper. She was carrying a big parcel wrapped in grease-proof paper and a bottle of lemonade.

'You look nice,' I said. 'Like a bumble bee.' And she laughed and started zooming round the kitchen making buzzing noises.

My mum and dad saw us off at the front door and after a big argument about whether or not I should take my anorak and a lot of boring advice about being careful and staying out of trouble and being home before dark we set off towards the river.

'I'll put my lunch in your bag, shall I?' said Angela, when we'd been walking for a bit. 'Then there'll only be one thing to carry and we can take it in turns. You can be first, if you like,' she added generously. The bag was heavy with her things in as well, but I didn't say anything and we walked on. When we reached the river Angela stopped and looked at me.

'Road or river bank?' she said.

'What?' I said.

'Well,' said Angela, 'We can either turn right here

and follow the road up to Barlow on this side of the river, or we can cross the bridge and walk up the bank on the other side. It makes no difference really, so I'll let you choose.'

'Let's cross here,' I said.

So we went over the bridge and started walking along the grassy bank towards Barlow, and it was all right for a little while. But the sun was hot and soon I started to feel a bit warm and uncomfortable in my thick polo-necked sweater. Apart from that the bag with the food in seemed to be getting heavier and heavier and the strap was starting to dig into my shoulder. Angela danced on ahead looking for water-rat holes in the bank and turning cartwheels in the grass.

'Come on, slowcoach!' she called. 'I'm leaving you behind.'

'The bag's heavy,' I grumbled. 'I think it's about time you had a turn at carrying it.'

'I don't mind,' she said cheerfully, and she carried it for a whole minute without complaining. Then she stopped and dumped it down on the grass.

'I've just had a good idea,' she said. 'If we eat our lunch now we won't have anything to carry except the empty bag.'

'But it's only about ten o'clock,' I objected.

'So what?' said Angela.

There was no answer to that. I can never think of anything to say when people say 'so what'. Besides, it seemed like a very long time since I'd eaten that egg for breakfast.

So we took off our socks and sandals and rolled up our trouser legs and paddled in the river for a while to cool off. Then we sat on the bank with our feet dangling in the cold water and ate our picnic.

'Swap some of your pâté sandwiches for a few of my

49

salmon ones?' suggested Angela. I shook my head hurriedly.

'No thanks,' I said. 'I'm not all that keen on salmon. But I'll swap a bit of ginger cake for some of your chocolate biscuits if you like.' We munched contentedly, and even my peanut butter tasted lovely in the fresh air. Some ducks came paddling by and we fed them the crusts. When every scrap was gone we finished our drinks and put all the rubbish into a litter bin. Then we set off again towards Barlow and it was nice not having that heavy bag to carry.

But we hadn't gone more than about half a mile when Angela started to lag behind. I looked round to see what had happened to her and she was sitting on the ground pulling off one of her shoes and socks.

'What's the matter?' I said. Angela made a face.

'A rotten old blister,' she said ruefully. I had a look at her heel and it looked pretty bad. I knew she wouldn't be able to walk much further.

'Well, it's your own fault,' I said. 'You shouldn't have worn your new shoes.'

'Thanks,' said Angela. 'That's what I call a very helpful remark.' She got to her feet. 'Come on,' she said. 'I'll just have to walk with one shoe off.'

We set off once more but I could see that Angela wasn't very happy. The ground along the river bank is all rough and littered with rocks and stones and she kept yelping with pain whenever she stepped on a sharp bit.

'There's Barlow bridge ahead!' she shouted suddenly, as we went round a bend in the river. 'We'll be there in two minutes, and then we can get the bus home.'

But when we got a bit closer we saw that it wasn't Barlow bridge we could see at all. It was only the railway bridge, and we realized that Barlow was still several miles away.

'Bother!' said Angela. 'It must be much further than I thought.' We stared at one another in dismay and walking to Barlow didn't seem like such a good idea after all. In any case, now that we'd eaten the picnic there didn't seem all that much point in going any further.

'Let's turn back,' I said. 'It'll be quicker than going on. We can always come another day when your foot's better.'

'Turn back?' said Angela. 'Turn back from an expedition? Don't be so pathetic. What would have happened to the North Pole and Mount Everest if Sir Walter Scott had turned back the minute he got a blister on his heel? I'm ashamed of you, Charlie Ellis.'

I had a feeling she was wrong about Sir Walter Scott, but I didn't say anything because she was looking up at the railway bridge and she had that look in her eyes. The one that always means trouble.

'We'll take a short cut,' she said.

'What do you mean?' I said. 'There's isn't a short cut. You can't be thinking of crossing the . . .'

'The railway bridge?' said Angela. 'Why not? You're not scared, are you?'

'Of course not,' I lied. 'But isn't it a bit dangerous? What if a train comes?'

'Don't be silly,' said Angela. 'There's only about three trains a day on Sundays.' She sat down on the grass and began to pull on her sock and shoe. Then she scrambled up the grassy bank towards the railway line, and there was nothing for me to do but follow.

We ignored all the signs saying PRIVATE BRITISH RAIL and PENALTY £100 and pulled ourselves up onto the line. It's only a single track that runs from Barlow to Edgebourne, so the bridge is very narrow, and there's a sort of concrete parapet a few feet high. Angela started to limp along between the rails and I walked behind her, stepping from one wooden sleeper to the next.

'What if a train comes now?' I said nervously, when we'd reached the middle of the bridge, and Angela giggled.

'We'd get squashed flat!' she said, and that was when we heard it, the rattle of wheels in the distance and the 'pah-pah' warning sound of a diesel train. At the same time I felt the rails give a sort of shudder under my feet and Angela turned round and flung herself at me in panic.

'What'll we DO?' she shouted.

There wasn't much space at the sides of the track, so I did the only thing I could think of. I dragged Angela with me and together we scrambled frantically off the line and up on to the concrete parapet.

We were only just in time. The train suddenly appeared round the bend and the bridge shook and trembled as it roared by. Angela and I clung together on the narrow ledge and it was ever so hard trying to keep my balance with the wind blowing Angela's hair in my face and her clutching at me and screaming in my ear because she's terrified of heights. She's so terrified of heights that when she played the part of Rapunzel in Mrs Moody's Christmas play and she had to climb up a ladder into the witch's tower, she was sick all over the stage.

Anyway, we swayed and wobbled on the edge of that parapet until the train had gone past and then suddenly we lost our balance. We fell backwards off the bridge, and plunged down into the river with an enormous splash.

It was horrible. The water was freezing cold and it closed right over my head and I went down and down and down until I thought I'd be sure to drown. But I started to kick hard with my feet and at last I bobbed back up to the top. I spat out a great mouthful of dirty Thames water and gulped at the lovely fresh air. Then I shook the wet hair out of my eyes and looked round for Angela. She was gasping and spluttering a little way away, but she was all right too, because she gave me a wave when she saw me. Luckily we are both good swimmers, so we set off for the bank, the one nearest home, and Angela did her super fast crawl that she got a badge and a certificate for at the school swimming gala, while I did my normal stroke which is a cross between a breast stroke and a sort of doggy-paddle.

We had almost reached the bank when Angela started shouting at me and pointing at something big that was floating downstream towards us.

'Look,' she called. 'A boat. It's capsized.'

It was a small sailing dinghy, the kind they call a Mirror. I knew it was a Mirror because it had a red sail and I've seen them sailing at Upper Thames Sailing Club, and anyway Angela has taught me quite a bit about sailing since she went on that holiday sailing course at Salcombe last year and found out all about it.

The dinghy was floating on its side with the mast and sail lying flat on the water. I couldn't see anybody on it or near it, but there was a man running up and down on the bank yelling something and waving his arms, and I could see a little boy in an orange life-jacket who seemed to be crying.

'To the rescue!' shouted Angela, and she started swimming towards the boat. When she reached it she grabbed the centre-board and hung on. The centre-board is that long wooden bit that sticks out of the bottom like a keel. I wanted to help too, so I swam after her and caught hold of the mast, but she told me to let go and throw her the jib-sheet.

'The what-sheet?' I said. I couldn't see anything that looked like a sheet. 'Do you mean the sail?'

'Not the sail, stupid!' said Angela.' The jib-sheet. It's the rope that's tied to the front sail. You'll have to get in the boat and find it. Then throw the end of it over the side of the boat towards me.'

I pulled myself along the mast to the boat and it was hard to find the rope she wanted because they were all tangled up and I couldn't tell which was which. Then when at last I did find the right rope it wasn't all that easy to throw it over the side to Angela because it was all wet and heavy and it kept slithering back down on top of me and the big knot in the end kept hitting me on the head. But at the fourth try I managed to get it over and Angela caught the end and shouted 'Got it!' Then I wriggled along to the stern to see what she was doing.

Angela was dragging herself out of the water onto the flat centre-board and leaning all her weight on it. She leaned backwards and pulled on the rope as hard as she could and I thought it was very clever of her because it worked and suddenly the sail popped up out of the water and the boat came upright. It rocked like mad for a minute, and I thought it was going to capsize again the other way, but it turned itself round to face the wind and then became steady.

There was a cheer from the bank and I could hear people clapping. I looked round and saw that a little crowd had gathered to watch the fun. Angela pushed her wet hair away from her face and grinned at me. Then she heaved herself onto the boat.

'Come on,' she said. 'You next.' She dragged me in over the stern and it was very difficult with all my wet heavy clothes on. I suddenly gave a loud wail as I realized I'd lost my nice blue canvas bag.

'You're not going to worry about a little thing like

that,' said Angela scornfully, when I told her. 'You're lucky to be ALIVE!'

The boat was full of water, so when Angela had sorted out the tangle of ropes in the bottom she handed me a yellow plastic bucket that was tied to the mast with a long piece of string.

'Bail!' she said. So I did, and when we'd emptied out most of the water Angela showed me where to sit in the front end and which bit of rope to pull and she sat at the back and steered with the tiller and we sailed that boat all by ourselves to the bank and it was great.

Somebody grabbed us as we came alongside and we were helped ashore. And it was lovely to be patted on the shoulder and praised and congratulated and treated like a hero even though my teeth were chattering like mad from the cold and the water was trickling out of my shoes.

The man who owned the boat was called Mr Bought-flower and he had a big ginger moustache that twitched crossly while he told us what had happened. I felt sorry for his little boy who was still sniffling miserably and looked as if he never wanted to see another sailing boat as long as he lived.

'We were all rigged and ready to sail,' said Mr Bought-flower. 'Then I left him for two minutes while I went for my life-jacket. All he had to do was stand on the bank and hold the boat. And the silly clot went and let go. Of course the first little gust capsized it, and it isn't half lucky you two came along when you did. The boat could have gone over the weir at Edgebourne by now.'

He stared at our dripping clothes. 'It's funny though. I never saw you jump in. Were you on the bank when it happened?'

Angela and I looked at one another.

'Oh, we were just passing by,' said Angela vaguely.

55

Mr Boughtflower insisted on driving us home in his car and we made big wet patches on his nice leather seats but he said it didn't matter, it was the least he could do. And my mum nearly had a fit when she saw me and said it was a stupid and foolhardy thing to do but I could see she couldn't help feeling a bit pleased and proud when Mr Boughtflower said what a fine brave clever girl I was and of course he made it sound as if we had jumped in the river on purpose to save his boat, and it was lucky he didn't know anything about the railway bridge because that would have been a bit difficult to explain.

Well, I had to have a hot bath and go straight to bed and my dad made me drink some hot milk with brandy in it and it was horrible and it made me choke and I still caught a rotten cold and had to miss a whole week of school and I couldn't even go to that nice David Watkins' birthday party that I'd been looking forward to for weeks. And it didn't seem fair somehow because of course Angela was perfectly all right and didn't catch a cold or miss the party or anything. But she did come to see me afterwards to tell me all about it, and she even remembered to bring me a piece of birthday cake.

6

IT's funny how my friend Angela always manages to get her own way. I don't know how she does it. I don't mean that she's spoilt exactly, but somehow whenever there's an argument about anything she always seems to get what she wants in the end. Like the time she wanted to be the Prince in the school pantomime. And that awful day when she went mad about a pair of red shoes.

It was a few days before the school term started and Angela and her mum came round to our house for coffee at about ten o'clock in the morning. Auntie Sally said she was taking Angela up to London to buy new school shoes and would we like to go with them.

'I thought it would be a nice outing for the girls,' said Auntie Sally to my mum. 'We could go up on the train, and have a snack lunch in a pub or something. What do you think, Liz?'

I love going to London and it doesn't happen very often so I was all excited and pleased.

'Oh, do let's go, Mum,' I begged. 'We haven't been to London for ages.'

'We can have tea in Harrods,' said Angela. 'With chocolate declares.'

'Well,' said my mum slowly, sipping her coffee. 'I don't know. I really ought to do some washing today.' But we all made such a fuss that she finally agreed.

'I'll come on one condition,' she said, giving me a hard stare like Paddington Bear. 'That you and Angela behave yourselves. I don't want a repetition of last time.'

I blushed and Angela giggled. Last time we were in Harrods, Angela and I had got bored with looking at furniture and had climbed into a big double bed when nobody was looking and had pretended to be asleep. And it was very funny because a whole lot of customers crowded round the bed and laughed like anything especially when Angela started to snore. But the manager didn't think it was funny at all. He was furious. He was so furious that he made us all leave the store and my mum said she had never been so humiliated in her life. But my dad roared with laughter when he heard about it and said it was something he had always wanted to do himself only he didn't dare. I don't know how I dared either, but somehow when you're with Angela she makes you dare anything.

'Oh, yes, Mum,' I promised. 'We'll behave ourselves this time. Won't we, Angela?'

'We'll be as good as gold,' said Angela, smiling sweetly, and she looked as if she really meant it.

She was dressed up to go to London and she looked lovely. She was wearing her best black velvet flared trousers and a red silky blouse with long sleeves. She had a matching black velvet bolero trimmed with red ribbon, and a red ribbon in her hair. Angela has more nice clothes than anybody else I know. Even Auntie Sally.

'Just give us a few minutes to change into something decent,' said my mum to Auntie Sally. 'I think there's a train at about eleven.'

Angela and I were as quiet as mice on the train because we saw Mr Lunnon getting into the same compartment and we didn't want him to see us. He's a very nice man actually, and he used to chat to us a lot, but I don't think he likes us any more after what we did to his notice. He has a sort of farm, you see, selling fruit and vegetables and things, and he had this sign on the gate which said 'Pick Your Own Strawberries'. Only Angela and I crept out late one night when everybody was asleep and changed it. I don't know how Mr Lunnon found out it was us but he must have done, because he doesn't talk to us any more and he scowls whenever he sees us. So I don't think he liked having a sign that said 'Pick Your Own Nose'.

It was after twelve when we got into the West End so we decided to have some lunch first before doing any shopping. We chose one of those nice London pubs with tables and chairs outside on the pavement where children are allowed and you can sit and have a drink and watch all the people going by. And it's lovely because you see all kinds of funny people in the oddest clothes, not a bit like they are in Edgebourne, and I once saw a man with all his hair shaved off and his head painted with green and yellow stripes. Honestly. Green and yellow stripes all over his head and down the back of his neck. And my mum said it was rude to stare but I just couldn't help it and anyway if the man didn't want people to stare why did he paint his head with green and yellow stripes?

We all sat down under a Martini umbrella and a waiter came out to take our order. He gave us a menu to look at and there were so many different kinds of sandwiches that I didn't know which to choose.

'What would you like, Charlie?' asked my mum. 'Look, they've got your favourite. Salmon and cucumber.'

I went red as Auntie Sally and Angela both stared at me in surprise.

'I thought Charlie was allergic to cucumber, said Auntie Sally, raising her eyebrows.

'And she's not all that fond of salmon, either,' said Angela, glaring at me suspiciously.

'Oh, that was ages ago,' I said weakly. 'People can change their minds, can't they? Anyway, I feel like a cheese and tomato roll and a packet of smoky bacon crisps and a coke.' The waiter wrote it all down and then smiled at Angela.

'And what about the other young lady?' he said.

'Half a pint of green slime and a packet of soggies, please,' said Angela sweetly, and I started to giggle.

The waiter blinked. 'I beg your pardon?' he said. 'I didn't quite catch . . .'

I gave Angela a kick under the table because I could see that my mum and Auntie Sally were beginning to look a bit cross and after all we had promised to behave ourselves.

'Ouch!' said Angela, and glared at me some more. 'A glass of lemonade and lime and a packet of cheese and onion crisps,' she said to the waiter. 'And a cheese and tomato roll, the same as HER.'

After lunch we walked along Oxford Street and the pavements were packed with people sightseeing and shopping and talking in all kinds of funny languages, and that's when Angela saw the shoes. They were resting on a satin cushion, right in the middle of a huge shop window, and they were the nicest shoes I have ever seen.

They were made of shiny red patent leather with black stitching and black heels and little black velvet bows on the front. There was a card propped against the cushion. It said 'Hand Made Children's Shoes From Italy'. There was no price ticket.

Angela clutched my arm and sucked in her breath and her eyes went all big and round.

'Ooh, Charlie!' she said. 'Just look at those shoes!'

'Come on, Angela,' said Auntie Sally impatiently. 'It's no use looking at those. We've come to get plain brown leather lace-ups for school, and that's all. Anyway, those are probably horribly expensive.' And she walked away into the shop with my mum, leaving Angela and me to follow. Angela gave the red shoes a last lingering glance and then trailed behind her mum into the shop.

She scowled all the time at the fair-haired young man in spectacles who came to serve us, and she was as unhelpful as anything when he kept bringing brown leather shoes for her to try on. I even saw her draw back her foot and kick him sharply on the shin once when nobody was looking, but he only winced a bit and said something under his breath.

At last a pair was found that fitted. The young man took the money and went away to wrap up the shoes. Angela looked at her mum and I could see there was going to be trouble.

'Mum,' she said loudly, and she sounded determined. 'Please, Mum. You could at least ask the price.'

Auntie Sally sighed. 'Well, I'll ask,' she said. 'If it'll make you feel any happier.'

'The red shoes in the window?' said the assistant when he came back. 'Oh, yes, madam. Charming, aren't they. They're hand-made especially for us in Turin. Twenty-seven pounds fifty, madam.'

Auntie Sally gave a little shriek. 'Good heavens!' she

said. 'That's quite out of the question, I'm afraid. Come along, Angela. You've got quite enough pairs of shoes as it is.'

Angela's mouth went all trembly.

'But I want THOSE shoes!' she wailed, and people were starting to turn round and stare at her. 'They go with my OUTFIT! My red blouse, and my black trousers, and my bolero, and EVERYTHING! I've never wanted anything so much in my whole LIFE!' Big tears started to roll down her cheeks.

'You needn't buy me a birthday present or a Christmas present EVER AGAIN!' she shouted. 'I'll even sell my new bike, if you want. Oh, Mummy, how can you be so CRUEL!' And she sank into a heap in the middle of the floor and began to howl and moan and sob and throw herself about.

Well, that was the first time I had ever seen her like that and I was taken in completely. I bent over her and patted her shoulder helplessly, and then I saw that it was all a big act because she took her hands away from her face for a second and winked at me.

My mum looked pink and embarrassed and Auntie Sally was looking really angry because everybody in the shop had stopped talking and they were all staring at Angela and pointing and tut-tutting and nudging one another and saying what a shame.

Auntie Sally took a deep breath and stepped grimly towards Angela, but I never found out what she was going to do because just then a woman screamed somewhere at the back of the shop and a small man in a dirty old jacket started to run towards the door with a big leather handbag clutched in his arms.

'Stop him! My bag! It's got all my money in it!' shrieked a fat lady in a fur coat, and it was easy to see how it had happened. The man had grabbed his chance while everybody was looking at Angela. He had snatched the lady's handbag and was now making a dash for the door, pushing people roughly out of his way. Everybody seemed to startled to move.

Everybody, that is, except Angela. As the thief ran past her she simply stuck out her leg in front of him. He staggered, lost his balance, and then reeled sideways into a big display of ladies' shoes. The shoes swayed about a bit and then toppled down on top of the man with a great crash. By the time he had picked himself up the manager and his assistant were ready to grab his arms and lead him away. And off he went, struggling and muttering, and I heard him say something about Angela which was very rude indeed. Miss Collingwood wouldn't have liked it at all.

It didn't bother Angela, though. She picked up the handbag, which had slithered away along the floor, and took it back to the fat lady who was shaking all over and had her hands pressed to her mouth. And of course once again Angela was the hero of the day.

'There's nearly five hundred pounds in that bag,' said the fat lady, sinking tearfully into a chair. 'I don't know what I'd have done if I'd lost it. My husband would have been so cross with me. He's always telling me not to carry so much money around with me.' She turned to Auntie Sally.

'It's your little girl, I believe,' she said. 'You must let me give her some kind of reward. Didn't I hear her saying something about a pair of red shoes?'

Auntie Sally shook her head. She still looked grim.

'No, really, I'd much rather you didn't . . .' she began firmly. But Angela was jumping up and down and her whole face was glowing.

'The shoes! The red shoes!' she said breathlessly.

Auntie Sally looked at my mum and my mum looked

at Auntie Sally. Then they both looked at Angela.

'No,' said Auntie Sally. But this time she didn't sound quite so firm and the fat lady quickly interrupted.

'Please, I absolutely insist,' she said. 'You must allow me to show my gratitude.' She turned to the fair haired assistant. 'The red shoes in the window, I think it was?' she said.

'Certainly, madam. At once, madam,' he said, and went rushing off. So to avoid another scene Auntie Sally had to give in. The assistant found a pair of red shoes in Angela's size and they fitted beautifully. She was so delighted with them that she refused to have them wrapped up. She danced out into the street wearing them and I was left to carry the bag with her old shoes in as well as the new brown leather ones.

But as we walked back along Oxford Street towards the tube station Angela took my arm and gave it a squeeze.

'I'll let you wear them too, sometimes,' she promised. And she looked so happy I could have hugged her.

7

ANGELA and I were late home from school one Friday afternoon because we stayed behind in the classroom to help Miss Bennett tidy the drawers of her desk. She keeps chalk and blackboard dusters and stuff like that in them, so they get as dusty as anything and have to be cleaned out all the time. Angela and I don't mind doing it though, because Miss Bennett always gives us each a gold star for helpfulness, and you have to stick the stars on a chart on the wall and when you've got ten stars you get a lovely gold badge to wear.

Everybody at school had been talking all day about a circus that was coming to Cookburn Green for the weekend, and on the way home through the village we chatted about it and about whether our parents would let us go.

'We can always ask,' I said. 'My dad might take us tomorrow night.'

'Tell you what,' said Angela. 'Why don't I come to your house for tea and then we can ask him together.'

I thought that was a good idea, because even my dad finds it difficult to say no to Angela. So when we reached our street she ran into her house to tell her mum she was having tea with me, and I went in our back door. I was so late that my dad was home already, and he was pacing up and down in the kitchen looking a bit anxious.

'There you are, Charlie,' he said, and he sounded pleased to see me. More pleased than usual, I mean. And sort of relieved as well.

'You're a bit late,' he said. 'Where've you been?'

'I stayed behind with Angela to tidy Miss Bennett's drawers,' I said.

My dad snorted with laughter. 'I bet they're long and pink with elastic round the knees,' he said.

'What are?' said my mum, coming into the kitchen and starting to clear my satchel and my dad's newspaper off the kitchen table.

'Miss Bennett's drawers,' said my dad, and my mum tut-tutted and said what a thing to talk about. My dad laughed again and ruffled my hair.

'Anyway, I'm glad you're home,' he told me. 'I was almost on the point of coming to look for you. Not that there's any real danger of course. It'll be miles away by now.'

I looked at him. 'What will?' I said. My mum picked up the kettle and pushed it into my hand and I think it was a hint that she wanted me to fill it.

'Thank heavens you're back, Charlie,' she said. 'We were beginning to get a bit worried with that lion on the loose.'

66

'What lion?' I said, but I still didn't get any answer because just then there was a frantic banging on the back door and sounds of shouting from outside. My dad opened the door and Miss Menzies rushed in, gasping for breatn and all her rolls of fat wobbling like jelly.

'Ooh, I can't bear it!' she said. 'Look at me! I'm all of a quiver. You'll let me stay here, won't you, Mr Ellis? Just until it's caught. I'm scared to death on my own. Suppose it breaks my door down or sticks its head through the window!' She shuddered and gulped and my dad made soothing noises and patted her shoulder and helped her into a chair.

'A nice cup of tea is what you need,' said my mum, and Miss Menzies nodded gratefully.

'Yes, please, Liz,' she said. 'You are kind. And perhaps I could have just a teeny piece of cake as well. I always get hungry when I'm frightened, and the thought of that great lion roaming around . . .' And she mopped her face with a big white hanky.

'What lion?' I said again, but nobody took any notice of me because they were all arguing about police messages and what time the news would be on the radio and whether it was likely to be on the telly as well.

'Will somebody please tell me what's going on?' I said in a loud voice, and they all stopped talking and turned round to look at me. My dad glanced at his watch and then went over to the radio and switched it on.

'Listen,' he said. 'It'll be on the news in a minute.'

There was a bit of music and then a man's voice said, 'Here is the six o'clock news.' We all went quiet to listen, and even Miss Menzies stopped talking for once. First there was a long boring bit about Parliament and the Commons and what the Prime Minister had said to the Leader of the Opposition and what the Leader of the Opposition had said to the Chancellor of the Exchequer and I stopped listening because I didn't want to know what any of them had said and I'm sure nobody else ever does either. And I think they should spend more time running the country instead of all this arguing and playing about the commons and I bet all they do there is play football. But then I pricked up my ears because the next bit was very interesting.

'Listeners in the Cookburn Green area of Buckinghamshire are warned that a young male lion escaped this afternoon from Antonio's Circus and was last seen moving towards the woods near the river. He is said to be quite tame and not likely to attack anyone, but listeners are warned that it would be extremely unwise to approach the animal and anyone who sees him is requested to contact the police immediately. The lion, whose name is Hercules, was being exercised on a leash when he broke away from his keeper. Police and circus officials are at present searching the area.'

Everybody started talking at once and then there was another bang on the back door and Angela burst in.

'Have you heard?' she said, and her cheeks were all pink with excitement. 'A savage man-eating lion is on the loose and we're all going to be gobbled up in our beds!' And she growled and snarled and pawed at Miss Menzies, who gave a shriek and cowered down in her chair.

'Stop that at once, Angela Mitchell!' said my mum sharply. 'Poor Miss Menzies' nerves are quite bad enough as it is. And if you've come for tea you'd better get Charlie to take you upstairs out of my way while I make it.'

It was a lovely sunny evening and I could tell by Angela's face that she wasn't very keen on staying indoors.

'Can't we play in the garden, Mum?' I said.

'Don't be silly, it's not safe,' said my mum, but my dad said he thought it would be all right providing we stayed close to the house.

'Cookburn Green is five miles away from here,' he said. 'And it's very unlikely that the lion will approach such a populated area. But don't go out of the garden, will you. It's better to be safe than sorry.'

Angela and I went outside and she ran straight down the garden to the playshed. When I got there she was leaning on the door and giggling her head off.

'What's the matter with you?' I said. 'What's so funny?'

'Charlie,' she said. 'This is going to be the funniest thing you ever saw. We're going to frighten Miss Menzies out of her wits.'

She went into the shed and started to drag out the dusty old fur rug from the floor.

'What are you going to do?' I said. But she only giggled some more and started heaving the rug down the path to the orchard.

Our orchard is nothing but a small patch of rough grass at the bottom of the garden and it's only got two apple trees and a few old blackcurrant bushes in it but my dad likes to call it the orchard. I like it because it's nice and quiet and peaceful there as our house is right on the edge of the village and there's only fields on the other side of the fence, and you can see the woods down towards the river. And in the winter when there are no leaves on the trees you can even see the river.

Anyway Angela dragged that old rug down into the long grass beside the fence and rolled it up into a sort of fat sausage shape. Then she came back to the shed and got busy with an old cardboard box and a pair of scissors.

'I wish you'd tell me what you're doing,' I said, but

she only shook her head and laughed. I watched as she cut out a round shape with two points sticking up on top like a pair of ears. Then she rummaged around in the cupboard until she found a length of old rope. She unravelled the end of the rope to make a sort of tassel. She took the cardboard shape and the piece of rope down to the orchard and I followed curiously. And it was only when she put the head at one end of the rolled-up rug and the tail at the other end that I saw what she had done.

'Angela!' I said, and my voice went all squeaky. 'You've made a lion!'

Angela started to dance up and down. 'Isn't it great!' she said. 'Doesn't it look real! I bet it looks as lifelike as anything from a distance.'

I didn't much like the idea of frightening Miss Menzies, and I knew my mum would have a fit as well, but the lion looked so funny that I couldn't help laughing.

'I think you're horrible,' I said. 'What a rotten trick!'

'Nonsense!' she said. 'It's only a joke. I can't wait to see their faces!'

Just then we heard my mum calling from the back door.

'Tea's ready, girls. Come and get it while it's hot.'

'See you later, Leo,' said Angela. She gave the lion a friendly pat on the back and we went in for tea.

Angela kept making funny faces at me over the table and I could hardly eat my fish fingers and chips for laughing but we got through them somehow. And Miss Menzies had two helpings of chips and two helpings of jam roly-poly pudding and custard and three cups of tea. Towards the end of the meal Angela got up from the table.

'Excuse me, Auntie Liz,' she said politely. 'May I get a glass of water, please?'

70

'Yes, dear,' said my mum. 'Of course you may. Just help yourself.' And Angela went over to the sink.

Our kitchen sink is right under the window that looks out onto the garden. Angela turned on the tap and glanced carelessly out of the window while she waited for her glass to fill. Then she gave a loud shriek that made me jump even though I was expecting it.

'The lion!' she shouted. 'Look! Auntie Liz! Uncle Ted! The lion's in your orchard!'

There was pandemonium at the table and Miss Menzies spilt a whole cup of tea into her lap. We all rushed to the window and looked out. The sun was going down and the garden was filled with a golden sort of light. Angela's lion looked as real as anything lying there in the long grass just as if it was asleep.

My mum shrieked and Miss Menzies started to wail and even my dad said 'Good Lord!' in an astonished sort of voice. I was surprised at my dad because I never expected him to be fooled for a minute, but he didn't have his glasses on and he can't really see all that far without them.

'Police,' he muttered. 'Must phone the police.' And he made for the hall with my mum and Miss Menzies at his heels, both talking at once.

'You've got us in a right mess now,' I said to Angela. 'The police will be here in a minute and they'll go in the garden and they'll find your lion and then there'll be an awful row.'

'No there won't,' said Angela, and she didn't look a bit bothered. 'Because I'm going down there now to hide everything. It'll only take a second.' She opened the back door. 'You stay here and make some excuse if anybody asks where I am,' she said.

As soon as she'd gone the grown-ups came back into

the kitchen. Miss Menzies and my mum both looked a bit calmer.

'The police are on their way,' said my dad. 'And somebody is coming from the circus as well.' He glanced round the kitchen. 'Where's Angela gone?' he said.

I waved my arm vaguely. 'Oh, I don't know. She was here a minute ago.'

My mum grabbed my arm and shook me hard. 'Where is she?' she said, in a wild sort of way. 'Don't tell me the stupid child has gone outside?'

They must have seen from my face that she had because my dad clutched at his hair and then started towards the back door. But before he reached it the door flew open and Angela fell inside. She slammed the door behind her and leaned her back on it and her hair was all over the place and she only had one shoe on. Her face was as white as anything and her eyes were huge and dark like pools of ink.

'Where've you been?' snapped my mum. 'What's the matter?'

Angela didn't speak. She just jerked her thumb over her shoulder and sort of rolled her eyes. I dashed to the window and looked out, and there it was. Sitting on the path near the back door. A lion. A real live one. It was huge and tawny-coloured with a dark mane and great big paws. It had a leather collar round its neck with a short piece of rope trailing from it. And it was playfully chewing Angela's shoe, just like a dog with a bone.

'The lion f . . . f . . . followed me!' gasped Angela. 'I lost my . . . my shoe!'

My mum gave a little scream and put her hand up to her throat and I thought for a minute that she was going to faint. But she swallowed hard and pulled herself together and just then there was a loud commotion out-

72

side. We all rushed to the window and saw that half a dozen policemen had arrived carrying big nets made of rope. There was a very thin dark-haired man with them and you could tell straight away that he was from the circus because he had a great big curly moustache and he was carrying a whip in his hand. And it was as exciting as anything and even better than the telly and we saw the lion start to back away when all those people appeared round the corner. But the man with the whip waved all the policemen back and crept towards the lion, talking to him softly in a gentle voice.

'Here, boy!' he said. 'Come on, boy. Come on, Hercules. Good boy. Come to Poppa.' And that great big lion pricked up his ears and trotted towards his master like a big friendly dog. The thin man quickly grabbed him by the collar and started to lead him away and the lion went with him as good as gold, but he wouldn't let go of Angela's shoe and it's lucky it wasn't one of her red patent leather ones that were hand-made in Turin.

My dad went outside as soon as it was safe and one of the policemen told him that the lion had been locked up in a van. Everybody heaved big sighs of relief, and even Angela soon got over her fright and started to look more like herself again. My mum put the kettle on and made a fresh pot of tea for the policemen and they all crowded into our small kitchen. The thin man came back after locking the lion in the van and it turned out that he was Antonio himself, the owner of the circus. He was as pleased as anything to have Hercules back unhurt and in good time for the show, and he kept shaking my dad's hand and laughing and saying what a clever idea it was. Nobody except Angela and me could guess what he was talking about, and then my mouth went all dry as one of the policemen brought in the bits of Angela's lion and dumped them in a heap on the kitchen floor.

Mr Antonio prodded them with his foot and chuckled.

'A decoy, no?' he said. 'A very clever idea. Like weeth-a ducks. And my Hercules, he theenk eez-a real!' He grinned round at us all and my mum and dad and Miss Menzies still looked blank.

'Who eez the clever one?' asked Mr Antonio. 'Who theenk-a that idea?'

Everybody looked at everybody else and then Angela stepped forward.

'It was me,' she said. 'I did it.'

Mr Antonio was delighted. He roared with laughter and patted Angela on the head.

'Such a leetle one, to be so clever!' he said. 'What I do now for you? I geeve you teeckets for show tomorrow, no?'

Angela's face went pink and her eyes went all sort of shiny. 'You mean free tickets?' she said, beaming.

Mr Antonio shook his head. 'No!' he said. 'I mean FIVE teeckets!' He took out his wallet and began to count out some tickets on the kitchen table. 'Uno, dos, tres, cuatro, theenko! One for Momma, one for Poppa, two for leetle girls, and one for the nice Grandmamma!'

We all thanked him and off he went, still grinning and chuckling, and I think he was the thinnest man I have ever seen. Even my dad said so. He said he reminded him of a filleted earwig.

I don't think Miss Menzies was very pleased at being mistaken for a grandma, but she was so delighted with her free ticket that she didn't complain at all. And they were all so relieved that everything had turned out so well in the end that they hardly even bothered to tell us off, although I bet Auntie Sally had something to say when Angela arrived home with only one shoe. Can you imagine trying to explain to your mother that the other one was chewed up by a lion?

Anyway, it was all worth it because the circus was great. We had the best ringside seats and the lions were fabulous, especially Hercules, and we all agreed that it was the best circus we had ever seen and even Miss Menzies enjoyed herself and had two choc-ices and a toffee apple.

But the best bit was right at the end when Mr Antonio made Angela come out of her seat into the middle of the ring and announced to the audience that she was the clever girl who had helped to capture Hercules when he escaped. And everybody cheered and clapped and stamped their feet and Angela blushed like anything and I was so proud of my friend I almost burst.

8

PLAYING tricks on people is Angela's favourite hobby. She even does it to me sometimes, and I'm supposed to be her best friend. Once she rushed into our house shouting 'Charlie! Quick! Come and see! There's a man walking down the street with no trousers on!' I went dashing out to have a look, but it was only Mr MacLennon in his kilt, and Angela fell about laughing when she saw my face. My dad thought it was funny too, but my mum said Angela was a very rude girl.

Angela does things like that all the time, so it's not really surprising that I thought her laryngitis was just another one of her jokes. It was a Monday morning, and when she called for me on the way to school she had her neck all muffled up in a woolly scarf. I asked her what

76

was the matter, but she could only talk in a hoarse sort of whisper and she told me she'd lost her voice.

Well, I looked at her and all I did was laugh. I was certain it was a trick, especially after what had happened on Friday, so I'd better tell you about that first.

That Friday had been a bad day for Angela, because she was in one of her talkative moods and you know how that always gets on teachers' nerves. My dad says that when Angela is in one of her talkative moods she's even worse than her mother. Anyway, Miss Bennett had to keep on telling her to shut up all day long, and by the last lesson, which was Nature Study, everybody was getting a bit fed up.

We were doing the Life History of the Frog, and the trouble was that Angela knew it all already. In fact the whole class knew it all already because we'd done the Life History of the Frog last year in Mrs Moody's class and the year before in Miss Whiteman's *and* the year before that in Miss Spender's, and it seems to me that you have to do the Life History of the Frog in every class in every school from the Kindergarten to the Sixth Form. Teachers get ever so flustered and upset if you say you've done it before so you have to let them get on with it and pretend it's all new and interesting. But I don't mind doing it all over again because I like drawing those funny little tadpoles with their wiggly tails and I'm getting quite good at them now.

Anyway, Miss Bennett had some baby tadpoles in a jar and she was holding them up in front of the class while she talked so that we could all see them.

'And then, after the eggs hatch out,' she said, 'the tadpoles feed on the jelly around them.' Angela bobbed up out of her chair.

'Please, Miss Bennett,' she said. 'I saw this programme on the telly the other day. And the man said they don't think that's true any more. Everybody used to think so, but now they've found out that the jelly is only a sort of protection, and the baby tadpoles feed on pondweed and possibly small organizations in the water.'

Miss Bennett sighed. 'I think you mean organisms, Angela,' she said. Angela nodded and sat down.

'Well, that's most interesting,' continued Miss Bennett. 'You can see how science is discovering new facts all the time. Now, where was I? Oh, yes. The young tadpoles breathe under water by means of —'

'Gills,' said Angela, bouncing out of her desk again. 'They're very interesting things, Miss Bennett, because they can absorb oxygen from the water.'

Miss Bennett frowned. 'That's quite correct, Angela,' she said. 'I'm glad you know so much about it. But I'd rather you didn't interrupt the lesson. There'll be plenty of time for discussion afterwards.' Miss Bennett looked down at the jar of tadpoles.

'Now, the hind legs develop first, and then the —' But Angela was on her feet again.

'I'm sorry, Miss Bennett,' she said. 'But the man on the telly said that all the legs develop at the same time. It only looks as if the hind legs develop first, because the front ones are hidden by the gill flaps.'

'Angela!' said Miss Bennett crossly. 'I have asked you not to interrupt. If it happens again I shall have to send you out of the room. I don't know what's the matter with you today.' Miss Bennett started to walk around the room, stopping at each desk to show us the tadpoles in the jar.

'This is the stage these tadpoles are at now,' she went on. 'They are growing very rapidly and need lots of food. We can even give them small pieces of meat to nibble and —'

'Excuse me, Miss Bennett,' said Angela, jumping up

yet again. 'But when we were in Miss Spender's class, Miss Spender said . . .'

Miss Bennett slammed the jar of tadpoles down on my desk with such a crash that some of the water slopped over the top. I watched the tadpoles wriggling with fright and I knew just how they felt.

'Angela Mitchell!' snapped Miss Bennett. 'I don't want to hear one more word from you today. You will please stand outside the door for the remainder of the lesson. And when you go home you will write out fifty times, "I must not speak until I'm spoken to" and bring it to me on Monday morning.'

I could tell by Angela's face that she was furious. Her mouth went all sulky and she stalked out of the room. I even thought she was going to slam the door, but there are some things that even Angela daren't do. She was still furious when school finished for the day and we started walking home together.

'That Miss Bennett is an old cat,' she muttered, with a scowl. 'I'm never going to speak to her again. Not ever!'

'Oh, Angela,' I said. 'You don't really mean that.' Angela stamped her foot in temper and pushed me away from her.

'You're pathetic,' she said. 'I most certainly do mean it. And if you were a proper sort of friend, YOU wouldn't speak to her again EITHER!'

We went home and I didn't see Angela at all on Saturday or Sunday because my mum and dad and I drove up to Newcastle that night to stay with my grandma, and she's my dad's mother and she's kind and fat and cuddly and she bakes the best stottie cakes in the North East. We didn't get back until very late on Sunday evening, so the next time I saw Angela was on Monday morning. And that was when she came round and told me she'd lost her voice.

Well, can you blame me if I didn't believe her? I looked at her suspiciously, and she had that sparkly look in her eyes that always means she's up to something.

'You haven't really lost your voice,' I said. 'Not really and truly. It's a trick. It's just so you won't have to talk to Miss Bennett, isn't it?' But she shook her head and pointed into her mouth.

'Laryngitis,' she whispered, and gave a husky sort of giggle, and I started to giggle too. I thought it was the funniest joke she had ever thought of, and I couldn't wait to see what happened when she tried it out on Miss Bennett.

So off we went to school and the first thing Miss Bennett said when we went into the classroom after prayers was 'Well, Angela? Did you do your lines?'

Angela smiled politely and nodded her head. She opened her satchel and put some sheets of paper on Miss Bennett's desk.

'Thank you, Angela,' said Miss Bennett. 'I hope this has taught you a lesson. We'll say no more about it, but I would like you to promise that it won't happen again.'

Angela opened and shut her mouth once or twice and made a funny little croaking sound. I had to stuff my hanky in my mouth to stop myself from laughing when she solemnly shook her head and pointed her finger down her throat.

'Can't . . .' she whispered, 'Can't talk.'

'Oh, dear,' said Miss Bennett. 'What's the matter, Angela? Have you lost your voice or something?' Angela nodded hard and Miss Bennett gave her a sympathetic little smile.

'Well, I'm sorry to hear that,' she said. 'But at least it means we'll all get some peace and quiet for a couple of days.' Everybody laughed when Miss Bennett said that, because it was a joke, and you always have to laugh at teachers' jokes. Angela went to her seat, blushing and scowling, and I heard Laurence Parker hiss 'Dummy!' at her as she went past.

'And now let's get on with our poetry lesson,' said Miss Bennett. 'We've wasted enough time this morning. I hope you've all learnt your poem over the weekend. Charlotte, will you please stand up and recite the first few lines of Wordsworth's "Daffodils".'

I got up and took a quick peep over my shoulder at Angela. And then I suddenly went cold all over because she was staring at me in a funny sort of way and telling me something with her eyes. I knew what she wanted me to do. She wanted me to prove that I was a proper sort of friend. She wanted me to pretend that I'd lost my voice too, so that I wouldn't have to speak to Miss Bennett either.

'Well, come along, Charlotte,' said Miss Bennett impatiently. 'You haven't forgotten it, surely?'

I gazed miserably down at my desk and thought if Angela was brave enough to do it then I must be too, or she would never forgive me. She would choose somebody else to be her best friend and it would probably be that awful Delilah Jones. I opened my mouth.

'I wandered lonely . . .' I whispered, and then stopped.

Miss Bennett stared at me suspiciously.

'What's the matter?' she said in a stern voice.

I pointed down my throat and shook my head, just as Angela had done. Miss Bennett looked from me to Angela and then back again.

'Charlotte Ellis!' she said sharply. 'This is quite ridiculous! You can't mean that you've lost your voice, too?'

I nodded dumbly and Miss Bennett's face went pink and some of the boys started to snigger.

'I'm afraid I find this very hard to believe,' said Miss Bennett icily. 'That you should both happen to lose your voices on the same day. I don't suppose either of you has a note from your doctor?'

I shook my head again and looked at Angela, expecting her to do the same. Now we're for it, I thought. But Angela was rummaging in her satchel and then I couldn't believe my eyes because she got out a small white envelope and took it to Miss Bennett with a polite smile. My heart sank into a big heavy lump at the bottom of my stomach.

Miss Bennett opened the envelope and read the note.

'This is indeed from Angela's doctor,' she said. 'It explains that Angela has a mild throat ailment and has lost her voice. It says that it is not serious or infectious, however, and she is quite well enough to attend school providing she stays indoors at break times.' Miss Bennett folded the note and glared at me over the top of her glasses.

'Well, Charlotte? I suppose you have a note from your doctor?'

I swallowed and croaked weakly, 'No, Miss Bennett.'

'And in fact you haven't lost your voice at all,' said Miss Bennett in an ominous sort of way.

I hung my head. 'No, Miss Bennett,' I said.

'Then what is your explanation for this strange behaviour?'

'It was ... it was a joke,' I mumbled. Everybody tittered and giggled and Miss Bennett looked round the room with a stern expression.

'I'm afraid none of us find that sort of joke in the least amusing, do we?' she said to the class. And they all stopped sniggering and shook their heads solemnly, and doesn't it make you sick the way everybody always agrees with the teacher?

'Charlotte, you will stay indoors at break time and clean out the art cupboard as a punishment,' said Miss Bennett. 'And you will please try to behave more sensibly in future.'

'Yes, Miss Bennett. Thank you, Miss Bennett,' I breathed gratefully. Cleaning out the art cupboard is a horrible mucky job and it makes your hands all filthy but it's a lot better than some of the punishments Miss Bennett manages to think up. So I felt I was quite lucky really and I didn't mind too much when everybody else trooped out to play at the end of the lesson. Anyway, it meant that I could stay indoors with Angela, and do you know, she didn't laugh a bit about me making such a right idiot of myself about the laryngitis, and she even started to help me tidy the cupboard. But that was when the other awful thing happened.

I was clearing out all the junk which had been shoved to the back of the cupboard when I came across an old battered tin. I heaved it out and looked at the label and it said Cow Gum. I laughed and showed it to Angela.

'I wonder if that's for sticking cows,' I said. Then I started to put it away again on one of the shelves but Angela leaned over and took it out of my hands. Her face had sort of lighted up and I could see that she'd had one of her wicked ideas.

'What are you doing?' I said anxiously. Angela found a stick and prised off the lid of the tin and we both looked inside. A thick layer of glue lay at the bottom, all sticky any shiny like varnish. Angela gazed at it for a minute, then she skipped away across the room with the tin in her hands. She stopped beside Miss Bennett's chair and started to dip the stick in the glue. I gave a shriek of horror.

'Angela! Don't!' I pleaded. 'Not Miss Bennett's chair!'

Angela turned and waved the stick at me. 'You're right,' she whispered hoarsely. 'I think I'll use it on a pig, instead.' She crossed the room quickly, and before I could even try to stop her she had scraped out a big dollop of glue and spread it all over the seat of Laurence Parker's chair.

She pushed the tin of glue back in the cupboard just in time because that moment the bell rang for the end of break and the other children started to come back into the classroom. That nosy Delilah Jones began to wrinkle her face and sniff as soon as she came into the room.

'What's that funny smell?' she asked. But Angela only shrugged her shoulders and looked blank, and I turned my back and went on putting all the stuff back in the cupboard. I didn't know what else to do.

When I had finished I went back to my place and sat down. I had a quick peep at Laurence Parker's chair and you couldn't tell there was glue on it at all. It only looked a bit more shiny than usual. Then I saw Laurence Parker come into the room so I put my head inside my desk because I just couldn't bear to watch him sit down.

I knew Miss Bennett had come in because all the chattering suddenly stopped and I heard everybody scuttling to their places.

'We're going to do some spelling now,' came Miss Bennett's voice. 'Take out your green spelling books, please, everybody. You may have five minutes to revise the twenty words we did last week, and then I'll test you on them.'

I grabbed my spelling book and when I put down my desk lid I saw that Laurence Parker was sitting in his place next to me and he hadn't noticed a thing. I looked over my shoulder, but Angela had her head down over her book and didn't look up.

It was all quiet for a few minutes while everybody except me practised their words and then Miss Bennett stood up.

'We'll start with the front row,' she said. 'I'll ask each of you to spell one word for me. Now, Delilah. You're first. Your word is, enough.'

And that awful Delilah Jones leaped up, looking all smug and pleased with herself. 'E,N,O,U,G,H,' she said, and Miss Bennett smiled at her and said 'Well done,' and you should have seen Delilah Jones smirking all over her silly face.

Well, it went all the way along the front row and then all the way along the next row and then it was our row and I started to get that horrible feeling in my stomach that's called butterflies and I don't know why it's called getting butterflies because I think it feels more like great big creepy crawly caterpillars. And it was my turn at last and Miss Bennett said 'Pneumonia, Charlotte,' and it was the hardest word on the list and I should have known Miss Bennett would save that one for me. Of course I knew how to spell it. But how could I think straight? How could anybody think straight if they knew that it was Laurence Parker's turn next and he was sitting there glued to his seat?

I stood up quickly. 'New what?' I said stupidly, and Miss Bennet's mouth went all squeezed up at the corners as if she was sucking a lemon.

'Pneumonia,' she said again.

'Um, er, N,E,W ...' I began and Laurence Parker gave a snigger.

'Sit down, Charlotte,' said Miss Bennett crossly. 'It's obvious you don't know it. You must write it out three times in your book and learn it for next week. Perhaps Laurence Parker can do better. Laurence? Pneumonia, please.'

There was a sort of horrible clatter as Laurence Parker got to his feet and I didn't know where to look because of course his chair was stuck firmly to the seat of his trousers and had got up with him. His face went all red and he swung around to try to see what was the matter, but that only made things worse because the legs of the chair crashed into the desk behind. Miss Bennett's face went as black as thunder and everybody stared like anything and there were a few smothered giggles but nobody dared laugh out loud.

'What on earth are you doing, boy?' snapped Miss Bennett and Laurence Parker started twisting about and trying to pull himself free but the chair was well and truly stuck.

'Laurence Parker! Come here AT ONCE!' shouted Miss Bennett. 'I will not tolerate this sort of clowning during my lessons!'

Laurence Parker hunched his shoulders and shuffled forward to the front of the class, clutching the chair to his bottom with his hands. He looked a bit like a fat old tortoise with its house on its back.

'I . . . I seem to have got stuck,' he stammered miserably, and Miss Bennett clucked and tutted and fussed. Then she put one hand on his shoulder and the other on the back of the chair and pulled.

There was a dreadful ripping noise and there stood Miss Bennett looking a bit surprised with the chair in her hand and hanging from the chair was a big piece of grey material. And there stood Laurence Parker looking even more surprised with a great big ragged hole in the seat of his trousers and you could see his blue and red striped Marks and Spencers underwear. Everybody stared in horror and the whole room went dead quiet and all you could hear was people breathing and that was when I started to laugh.

It wouldn't have been so bad if it had been a quiet little giggle, or a subdued sort of chuckle, but it wasn't. It was a horrible loud cackle. My dad says that when

I laugh I sound like an old hen laying an egg. And I always seem to laugh at the wrong time and in the wrong place and sometimes it gets me into terrible trouble but I can't help it. Like the time at the vicar's garden party when Miss Menzies sneezed and her false teeth flew out and landed in the bowl of fruit punch. And that other time when we went to my Auntie Fiona's wedding up in Gateshead and my grandad trod on the end of the bride's long white veil as she was walking down the aisle and yanked it clean off her head and I laughed so much that I was sent out of the church and had to wait outside in the car so I missed the whole thing.

Anyway, Laurence Parker looked so funny standing there with that great hole in his trousers that if I hadn't laughed I'd have burst. My eyes streamed with tears and this time it was no use stuffing my hanky in my mouth because it only made me choke and laugh even more. And then of course when I started laughing like that it set everybody else off as well and soon the whole class was laughing like anything and you should have heard the din.

Miss Bennett started to thump on her desk with her fist and I knew I was in bad trouble because she only does that when she's really mad. And when I saw the way she was glaring at me I wished I hadn't laughed so much because of course that was what made her think it was me who had been messing about with the rotten old glue.

'There is glue on this chair,' said Miss Bennett, sort of quietly and ominously. 'And I don't have to ask who is responsible for this outrage.' Her eyes bored into me and I felt my face go scarlet. 'There were only two people left in this room at break time, and one of them has guilt written all over her face.' Miss Bennett turned to Laurence Parker, who had backed up against the wall to hide his underwear and was standing there looking daggers at me.

'Laurence,' she said, quite gently. 'You had better go and wait in the boys' changing room. I'm going to phone your mother and ask her to bring you a spare pair of trousers.' Then she turned back to me and her voice would have frozen the Sahara Desert. 'Charlotte Ellis, you will stay behind after school this afternoon. You and I must have a very serious talk.'

Well, of course I sort of hoped that Angela would stand up and confess, but I must admit I wasn't all that surprised when she didn't because I know what she's like. And I didn't get a single chance to speak to her on her own for the rest of that day, as she had to stay indoors again at lunch time because of her sore throat. So when four o'clock came everybody went home and I had to stay behind and get told off, and it was awful because Miss Bennett went on and on at me until I thought she'd never stop and all I could do was stand there and say nothing because of course she knew that it could only have been me or Angela and I couldn't tell on my friend, could I? Even if she did deserve it.

When at last she let me go and I escaped out of the school door, who should be waiting for me at the gate but Angela, and she had waited for me in the cold all that time. But when she squeezed my arm and whispered that I was the best friend in the whole world I pressed my lips tight together and walked away from her, because this time she'd gone too far and at least she could have taken a bit of the blame.

And then when I got home I suddenly felt a whole lot better, because my dad was there. And I told him all about it because I always tell my dad everything, and he said I was quite right not to tell on my friend. But he said Angela was a right little minx and it was high time

I gave her the push and found myself a new best friend who wouldn't keep getting me into trouble.

I thought about that, and in the end I made up my mind that he was right. I even managed not to speak to Angela for three whole days.

But somehow life is never so much fun without her, and when she came round on the third day, looking as sorry as can be and carrying her favourite picture of Elton John as a peace offering, I couldn't help feeling glad to see her and I hadn't the heart to stay cross with her any longer.

9

WHEN we went into the classroom one afternoon in December we found that a big clothes-hamper had been delivered during the lunch break. We all crowded round it to have a look, but Miss Bennett came in and shooed us back to our places.

'No lessons this afternoon, children,' she said, smiling. 'This hamper contains all the costumes for our Christmas play. We're going to have a look at them, and then I'll give you your parts.'

There was a buzz of excited chatter and everybody stared at Miss Bennett expectantly. Every Christmas each class has to do a play or a concert for the rest of the school, and we all look forward to getting dressed up and acting on Miss Collingwood's big stage. This year we had decided to do Cinderella, and we were all dying to know which parts we were going to play.

'We've been very lucky indeed this year,' said Miss Bennett. 'You probably all know Miss Reeder, the head-mistress at Dormund Grange? She came here to give out the prizes last Sports Day. Well, she happens to be a friend of mine, and when I told her that we were planning to do Cinderella, she very kindly offered to let us borrow the costumes they used last Christmas. I think you will agree that they are quite magnificent.'

Dormund Grange is a posh school for girls at Barlow and it's got a swimming pool and a gymnasium and a science laboratory and they play lacrosse instead of hockey so you can tell how posh it is. Your dad has to pay an awful lot of money for you to go there, and it's full of rich girls with pink bicycles and paddocks full of ponies and braces on their teeth. Angela says they're all snobs and they eat their mince and cabbage with silver knives and forks, so I knew that the costumes from their Christmas play wouldn't just be any old rubbish, and I was right.

Miss Bennett started to pull the things out of the hamper one at a time. There were silks and satins and velvets and brocades and sequins and lace and frills and embroidery and feathers and cloaks and swords and hats and shoes and buckles and belts and everybody went 'ooh' each time Miss Bennett held something up for us to see. She draped them all over the desks and chairs and soon the classroom began to look like a Carnaby Street boutique.

But the best costume of all was the one for Prince Charming. There was a white frilly shirt with long sleeves and little pearly buttons on the cuffs. There were white tights and a short black velvet tunic with a silver belt. There was a black velvet cloak lined with white satin, black shoes with big silver buckles, and a lovely black floppy velvet hat with a huge white ostrich feather. I peeped round at Angela and you should have seen her face. She was almost drooling.

'Now, I've made a list of all the parts,' said Miss Bennett. 'You're all going to be in it, so I hope everybody will be satisfied. First of all, the part of Prince Charming. I've chosen Charlotte Ellis.'

I couldn't believe my ears. I was so thrilled I could hardly speak. I got to my feet and beamed at Miss Bennett.

'Thank you, Miss Bennett,' I breathed. 'Thank you very much.' Suddenly a chair scraped on the floor behind me and I looked round. Angela was standing up and her face was as black as thunder.

'Excuse me, Miss Bennett,' she said. 'But do you think that's quite fair? Wouldn't it be better to draw the names out of a hat or something? I'm sure lots of other people would like the chance to be the prince. It's a lovely costume and . . .'

'Sit down, Angela,' interrupted Miss Bennett. 'I've chosen the parts very carefully, and I think Charlotte will make a splendid prince. She's tall and slim and she has nice short hair. She'll be just right.'

'But Miss Bennett,' said Angela. 'I'm just as tall as Charlie and just as slim and I'm sure she won't mind if . . .'

Miss Bennett was shaking her head firmly. 'Please stop arguing, Angela,' she said. 'Anyway, I'm sure you'll be quite happy when you hear which part I've given you. I want you to be Cinderella. Look at the lovely ball gown you will wear in the ballroom scene.' She held up a georgeous white dress all covered in frothy lace and I thought Angela would be pleased. But she scowled harder than ever.

'I'm fed up with always being the princess and wearing soppy dresses all the time,' said Angela in a loud voice, and everybody stared at her for daring to talk to Miss Bennett like that. Miss Bennett must have been in a specially good mood or even Angela wouldn't have got away with it. 'I was the princess in Miss Whiteman's play and I was Rapunzel last year in Mrs Moody's and you know I was sick on the stage.' She changed her tone to a pleading one. 'Let me be the prince this time, Miss Bennett,' she said. 'Please!'

'Angela, I have already made up my mind,' said Miss Bennett, and her voice sounded final. 'You will play the part of Cinderella, or nothing at all. It's entirely up to you. Anyway, whoever heard of a Prince Charming with hair nearly down to his waist? It would be silly.'

Angela's face was scarlet. She sat down, and she didn't say anything more, but I knew she was livid. And then that fat Laurence Parker stood up.

'Please, Miss Bennett,' he said. 'Why does it have to be a girl, anyway? Why can't it be a boy? I'd quite like to be the prince, too.'

The thought of that fat lump playing the part of Prince Charming nearly made me choke, and even Miss Bennett had to smile.

'No, Laurence,' she said. 'I want us to do this as a traditional pantomime. And in a traditional pantomime the part of the Principal Boy is always played by a girl, and the Dame is always a boy. I've got you down as one of the Ugly Sisters, and I'm sure you'll be just splendid.'

Everybody laughed and Laurence Parker groaned and pulled terrible faces, but I could see he was pleased because he always likes to act the clown.

'Now, everybody,' said Miss Bennett firmly. 'We've wasted quite enough time with all this wrangling. I'm going to read out the rest of the parts and I don't want any more arguments. Or any more tantrums,' she said, looking hard at Angela, who stared back with a stony expression.

Angela refused to speak to me at home time, and it wasn't fair because it was hardly my fault. When I tried to link arms with her she shook me off, and she walked a few yards behind me all the way home. She sulked for the whole of the weekend and didn't come round to play with me once.

But on Sunday evening I was sitting at the kitchen table doing my homework when there was a knock at the back door. Well, I was supposed to be doing my homework, but I was actually writing a letter to my Uncle Barrie, and I had made up a funny poem to put in it.

'There was a young lady called Nelly
Who gobbled a plateful of jelly
Some rhubarb and custard
And sausage and mustard
Which gave her a pain in the kneecap.'

I was having a good giggle at this when Angela marched in. She had a thin white box under her arm.

'Hello, Charlie,' she said, all friendly, as if nothing had happened. I was very pleased to see her, I can tell you. The weekend had been as boring as anything without her, and I was glad that she'd got over her sulks.

'Hello, Angela,' I said. 'Do you want to read my poem? It's very funny.'

'No, thanks,' she said, waving away my bit of paper. 'We've got more important things to do. Guess what's inside this box?'

I looked at the box but I couldn't think what might be in it. It could be anything. You never know with Angela.

'Chocolate peppermint creams?' I said hopefully, but she shook her head. Just then my mum came into the kitchen.

'Oh, hello, Angela,' she said. 'I'm just going to make some cocoa. Would you like a cup?'

'No thank you, Auntie Liz,' said Angela politely. 'And Charlie doesn't either. We're just on our way upstairs.' She tugged at my arm and I followed her up to my room, wondering what it was all about. She sat down on my bed and opened the box and I stared. In the box was a long pair of shiny steel scissors, and they looked very sharp.

'My mum's dressmaking scissors,' explained Angela in a whisper. 'She doesn't know I've got them. She'll kill me if she finds out.'

'But what do you want them for?' I said. I couldn't imagine what she was up to. Angela looked up at me.

'My hair,' she said.

I went cold all over.

'What about your hair?' I said.

'You're going to cut it off for me,' said Angela. 'You're going to cut it really short. As short as yours. Then Miss Bennett will have to let me be the prince in the pantomime.'

'No, Angela,' I said hurriedly, backing away from the scissors. 'I won't do it. I couldn't. Your lovely hair. You must be mad.'

Angela stood up. 'All right,' she said. 'If you won't do it then I'll just have to do it myself. And then it's sure to be a mess.' She walked stiffly to the bedroom door.

'Thank you, Charlotte,' she said, and it was the first time in my life she'd ever called me that. 'Now I know exactly what sort of a friend you are.'

'Don't go,' I said. 'I'll do it. If you really and truly want me to.'

Angela at once became all smiles. 'I knew you wouldn't let me down, Charlie,' she said. 'Come on then. Let's get it over with.'

She dragged my dressing table stool into the middle of the room and sat down on it. I picked up the scissors and I could feel my hands beginning to shake.

'I won't look until you've finished,' she promised. 'But make it good and short, won't you.'

I took a tress of her silky golden hair in my fingers and went snip with those sharp scissors. The lock of hair dangled from my hand like a shiny snake and I dropped it quickly on the floor.

'Get on with it!' said Angela impatiently. 'What're you mooning about for?'

So I took a deep breath and started snipping away at the sides and back until all her hair lay in great soft heaps on the carpet. I left the fringe alone because it was quite short already, but I cut the rest as short as I dared. When I'd finished I stepped back to look at her and I nearly cried.

It was awful. It really was. The back had somehow turned out shorter than the sides and there were funny little tufts sticking out round her ears. Some very short bits on the top were sticking straight up in the air. She looked a mess.

'I'm sorry, Angela,' I said nervously. 'It's not very good.' I quickly put the scissors back in the box and closed the lid.

'Never mind,' said Angela. 'At least it's cut. Let's have a look at it.' She got up and went to the mirror on my dressing table. She took one look and then let out a horrible shriek. She clutched her head in her hands and wailed and stamped her foot.

'I look AWFUL!' she shouted. 'What have you

DONE!' She swung round to face me and she almost spat.

'Charlie Ellis!' she hissed. 'You stupid IDIOT! I'll never speak to you again as long as I live!'

And then she flounced out, and the whole house echoed with the sound of the front door slamming.

I was miserably picking up the bits of hair when I heard Auntie Sally's voice downstairs. She was ranting and raving and sounded as cross as anything. I heard my mum trying to calm her down and after a few minutes my dad called up the stairs.

'Charlie, will you come down here a minute? Auntie Sally wants a word with you.'

I crept along the landing to the bathroom and locked myself in. After a while my dad came to look for me and he knocked on the bathroom door.

'I think you'd better come out, Charlie,' he said. But I didn't dare. I kept the door locked until he went away. I stayed in there as quiet as a mouse until at last I heard voices calling goodbye and I knew that Auntie Sally must have gone home. So I tiptoed back to my room and undressed as fast as I could and crawled into bed. I pulled the blankets right over my head and squeezed Benjamin tight, and when my mum came into my room a bit later I pretended to be fast asleep.

I think it's always better to stay out of their way until they've had time to cool off a bit if you possibly can. They can't stay mad for very long, and sure enough the next morning my mum and dad weren't cross with me at all, and anyway they'd known all the time that it must have been Angela's idea. But Auntie Sally had already been on the phone to say I would have to walk to school by myself. She was taking Angela for a rescue operation, she said, and would be bringing her to school later in the morning.

So I walked to school on my own, and when I got there everybody wanted to know where Angela was. I felt a bit uncomfortable and I didn't fancy trying to explain what had happened, so I pretended to know nothing about it. But I think Auntie Sally must have phoned Miss Bennett because she kept giving me funny looks all morning.

Anyway, we were all in the middle of a maths lesson when the door opened and in sailed Angela looking radiant. And everybody gasped because she looked absolutely fantastic. She had been to Mr Peter at Shampers and everybody knows he's the best hairdresser for miles around and my mum says he's dishy as well. My dad said dishy or not, that man certainly knows how to drive a pair of scissors and it's true.

Angela's hair had been trimmed and shaped close to her head like a shiny golden cap. Her ears peeped out like pink shells and she had soft feathery bits on her cheeks. She looked a bit like a pixie, and I could see that if anybody would make a perfect Prince Charming it was her. Everybody stared in silence and then Miss Bennett got up from her desk and took both Angela's hands in hers.

'Oh, Angela,' she said, and I thought that she was going to cry. 'What have you done to your beautiful hair?'

And so of course Angela got the part of Prince Charming after all. Miss Bennett explained that such an act of sacrifice for the sake of art just couldn't be ignored, and my dad said art his foot, Angela was a little madam who would go to any lengths to get her own way.

But everybody thought she made a lovely prince, and she really did look great in that black cloak with the satin lining and the big black hat with the ostrich feather. And I tried not to mind too much, because Miss Bennett let me play Buttons which was nearly as good, although the costume wasn't half as nice.

I've never seen anything so funny as David Watkins and Laurence Parker as the two Ugly Sisters, but there was one thing that spoiled the whole pantomime because you'll never believe me when I tell you who Miss Bennett chose to be Cinderella. That awful Delilah Jones!

10

THE worst thing Angela and I ever did was when we set fire to her dad's garage. And that was the day I nearly fell out with Angela for ever and ever. This is how it happened.

It was a nice sunny Saturday afternoon and Angela and I were sitting on a rug on her front lawn cutting pictures of Prince Charles out of magazines and sticking them in her scrap-book. She's got this idea that she's going to marry Prince Charles when she grows up, because he's going to be the next king of England, but I told her she'd have to learn how to ride horses and play polo first, and anyway she's not very keen on dogs so I don't know how she thinks she'll get on with all her mother-in-law's Corgis.

My mum and Auntie Sally had gone shopping together and my dad was up the ladder cutting the hedge between our two drives. We could see his head and shoulders above the hedge, and he kept grinning at us and waving the shears and shouting funny things at us to make us giggle. It was lovely and warm and peaceful.

At about half past two Uncle Jim came out of the house wearing shorts and tennis shoes and carrying his racquet.

'Keep an eye on the girls, Ted, will you,' he said to my dad. 'I'm just off to my match.'

He opened the garage door and backed out his shiny new Morris Marina. It was only six weeks old and he was always cleaning and polishing it and patting it as if it was a dog. Auntie Sally said that if she got as much loving care and attention as that car did she would be the happiest woman in the world, and Uncle Jim said that no doubt she did when she was only six weeks old but it was probably so long ago that she couldn't remember.

Uncle Jim left the car in the drive with the engine running while he came back to shut the garage door. but as he was pushing it shut the door fell off its hinges with a loud clatter.

'Dammit!' said Uncle Jim, giving the door a kick. You see, they had this really ancient tumble-down garage, made of wood and separate from the house, and it was so old and rotten that it was falling to bits. Auntie Sally kept nagging Uncle Jim to build a new one, but he said he was waiting until his bank manager was in a good mood.

Anyway, when my dad saw what had happened to the garage door he laughed so much he almost fell off the ladder.

'It's high time you did something about that wreck of a garage, Jim,' he said. 'I'd set fire to it if I were you. Sort of accidentally on purpose, if you know what I mean. Get the insurance company to pay for a nice new one.'

Uncle Jim made a face. 'Wish I dared,' he said. He propped the garage door against the side of the house, then he got into his car and drove away, giving us a wave out of the car window as he went.

I waved back but Angela hardly seemed to notice him going. She was gazing at the garage in a very thoughtful sort of way.

'Charlie,' she said suddenly. 'I've just had the most marvellous idea!'

'Oh, yes?' I said. 'What's that?' I looked at her and I didn't feel at all comfortable, because her eyes had gone all wide and blue and innocent, and that's when she's at her most dangerous.

'We're going to burn down my dad's garage,' she said, and a horrible shiver went down the back of my neck.

'What, now?' I said stupidly.

'Of course, now!' she said. 'I don't mean next week or next month. Now! While everybody's out.'

'Don't be silly, Angela,' I said. 'We'll get into awful trouble.'

'No we won't,' she said. 'We can make it look like an accident. Oh, come on, Charlie. Don't be such a bore. Think how pleased my dad will be. He'll be able to claim on the insurance and build a super new one.'

'Will he?' I said doubtfully.

'Of course,' said Angela. 'Didn't you hear what your dad said?' I shook my head.

'He was only kidding,' I said. 'I'm sure he was.'

'Well, maybe he was,' said Angela. 'But it's true all the same. You know when the old Barlow cinema burned down last year? The owners got a hundred thousand pounds insurance money, and they rebuilt it better than it was before. It was all in the paper.' I still wasn't convinced.

'But if it's as easy as that,' I said, 'why hasn't your dad set fire to it himself?'

'Oh, he's just scared,' she said. 'But we're not,' she added, giving me a look. 'Are we?'

'Er . . . no,' I said. 'Of course not.' I got up slowly. 'But my dad'll see us,' I said. Angela looked at her watch.

'Oh, we'll soon get him out of the way,' she said, as if he was nothing but a bothersome insect. She walked over to the hedge and looked up at my dad who was still snipping away at the privet.

'Uncle Ted,' she said. 'Isn't it nearly time for Wimbledon on the telly?'

My dad peered at his watch. 'Good Lord!' he said. 'So it is. Thanks, Angela.' And he scrambled down the ladder and disappeared indoors. Angela turned to me.

'See?' she said. 'Easy!'

I didn't like any of it one bit, but at the same time I couldn't help being sort of fascinated with the idea. So I followed Angela down to their shed, where she started to rummage around collecting old newspapers and bits of rag.

'Shouldn't take much to get it started,' she said. 'It's as dry as tinder. But there's no harm in making sure.' And she dragged out the big blue container of paraffin that Uncle Jim uses for his greenhouse heater in the winter.

She began to cart all the stuff to the back of the garage and I stood around watching helplessly for a bit until she gave me one of her looks.

'Well, aren't you going to give me a hand?' she said. I suppose I should have tried to stop her, but it wouldn't have been much use. You know what she's like once she gets an idea into her head. So I picked up some of the rags and paper and began to help her to stuff them into all the small gaps between the wooden boards along the back of the garage, and then Angela sprinkled a good dollop of paraffin all along the row from the blue container and it smelled awful.

'Right,' said Angela. 'All we need now it a match.' We looked at one another blankly, and Angela pondered for a minute.

'We don't have matches in our house,' she said. 'We're all electric.'

'So are we,' I said quickly. 'We don't keep any matches either.'

'Charlie Ellis!' said Angela. 'What a fib! Everybody knows your dad smokes like a chimney. He's always puffing away at that smelly old pipe. You know he's got matches.'

She was right. My dad smokes the sort of pipe that goes out every two minutes and he spends more time lighting it than he does smoking it. My mum says he smokes more matches than tobacco.

'Well, he might have some,' I admitted. 'But I can hardly just walk in and ask him for them, can I?'

'You'll have to sneak in and take them,' said Angela. 'They're bound to be lying around somewhere.' I gazed at her miserably.

'Go on, then,' she said. 'What are you waiting for?' So I trailed off round the corner and let myself in quietly at the back door.

The living-room door was open and it looked all cool and dim and inviting in there because my dad had pulled the curtain across the sunny window to get a better picture. He was sitting in his favourite armchair in front of the telly with his back to the door and Wimbledon was on and it was all sort of soothing with only the bonk bonk of the tennis balls and the odd spattering of applause and the quiet voice of the commentator, and all I wanted to do in the world was to curl up beside my dad and watch the tennis and forget all about Angela waiting outside for me to help her burn down her father's garage.

I stood at the door for a minute and when my eyes got used to the gloom I saw that my dad's pipe was lying in the ashtray on the coffee table next to his chair. And beside the ashtray was a box of matches.

I crawled over the carpet on my hands and knees until I was just behind my dad's chair. Then I slowly reached out my hand and ever so gently lifted the box of matches from the table. I had just started to crawl carefully backwards towards the door when the stupid matches made a tiny rattling noise and my dad's head suddenly came round the wing of the chair.

'Charlie?' he said, making me jump. 'Is that you?' I quickly put the matches behind my back and stood up.

'Yes, Dad,' I said. 'I came in to see who's winning.' I felt myself blush all over because it's horrible to tell fibs to your dad and it's something I hardly ever do. He stared at me.

'You're looking very surreptitious,' he said.

'Syrup what?' I said. It sounded like some kind of treacle tart.

My dad laughed. 'Surreptitious,' he said. 'You know. Suspicious. As if you were UP to something.'

'Who, me?' I said. 'Oh, no.' I fidgeted a bit and then said. 'Er . . . well. I'll just er . . . leave you in peace.' And I made for the door.

'O.K.' said my dad. 'And it's Bjorn Borg, if you really want to know.'

'What is?' I said.

'Bjorn Borg,' said my dad patiently 'He's winning. You came in to find out.'

'Oh,' I said. 'Oh, yes. So I did. Bjorn Borg, eh? How interesting. I'll just go and tell Angela,' I said, and escaped as fast as I could and flew round the corner to where Angela was pacing up and down impatiently. Her eyes brightened when she saw the matches and she almost snatched them from my hand.

I could smell the stink of paraffin as soon as we went round to the back of the garage and it made me start to cough. Angela knelt down beside the soaking rags and I suddenly realized what a terrible thing we were doing.

'Angela!' I said fearfully. She sat back on her heels and looked up at me.

'What's the matter, Charlie?' she said. 'Do you want to be the one to light it? Here you are, then.'

I shook my head hurriedly and started to back away, but she pressed the matches into my hand and gave me a little push. I knew she was dying to light it herself and it must have cost her a great effort to offer to let me do it so how could I refuse?

I knelt down and my hands were shaking so much that the first two matches didn't strike, they only broke in half. But the third one gave a little splutter and burst into flame and I dropped it quickly among the paraffin-soaked rags.

We both jumped back out of the way because there was a sudden sort of whoomph as the fumes ignited and blue flames began to lick along the ground at the bottom of the garage. We stood and stared for a bit and we heard the wood start to crackle.

'Come on, Charlie,' said Angela. 'We've got to get rid of the evidence.' And she picked up the paraffin container and set off towards the shed.

We were about halfway down the garden when we heard the sound of a car engine and Angela dropped the paraffin can in fright.

'Oh, no!' she breathed. 'My dad's back already!'

We dashed towards the gate and there was Uncle

Jim's blue Marina just turning into the drive. We waved at him frantically to try to make him stop, but he only tooted the horn at us and drove straight past, and he couldn't have noticed any of the smoke or anything because he drove his brand new car straight into the burning garage.

Uncle Jim got out of the car and slammed the door. He came towards us and he looked cross.

'The match was cancelled,' he said. 'Harry didn't turn up.' But we hardly heard what he said. We were both staring over his shoulder at the garage roof because flames were starting to lick along it towards the front and clouds of smoke were billowing from the sides.

'What's the matter with you two?' said Uncle Jim, and he turned round to see what we were staring at. I thought he was going to faint because he sort of staggered, and I used to think it was only in books that people tore their hair but that's what he did.

By now the roof of the garage was blazing merrily and there was a steady crackling sound. Smoke was pouring into the drive from the open doorway and you could hardly see the back of the car.

'My CAR!' shouted Uncle Jim. 'My NEW CAR!' And he started towards the fire. Angela clung to his legs and screamed, but he managed to disentangle himself and he disappeared into the smoke.

I don't think I have ever been so scared in my whole life. Angela and I didn't know what to do. We clung together and shrieked for help and it was horrible because we heard Uncle Jim trying to start the engine but it wouldn't start and the flames were leaping higher and higher and people were starting to come out into the street to see what was going on.

Well, at last Uncle Jim managed to get the car started. He backed it out into the street and it was black all over with soot but at least it was safe and Angela was nearly crying with relief because her dad was all right. And he was only just in time because just then the roof of the garage collapsed with a great crash and a shower of sparks. My dad suddenly appeared round the corner and what he said made us giggle hysterically.

'Holy smoke!' he said. 'What in blazes is going on!'

He went straight over to Uncle Jim who was leaning against the car watching the blaze with his mouth open and he had streaks of soot on his face and hands and he looked like something out of the Black and White Minstrel Show. One of the neighbours must have phoned for the fire brigade because suddenly we heard a siren in the distance and that was when Angela and I decided it was time for us to disappear. We sneaked away round the corner to my garden and shut ourselves in the playshed.

We sat there for a long time and we didn't speak a word. We didn't even look at each other. We just sat side by side on a couple of old crates and gazed at the floor and listened to all the commotion going on next door. There was a lot of shouting and people dashing about and then we heard a great hissing noise and the sound of running water. After a while everything went quiet and we heard footsteps approaching the shed.

'Charlie! Angela! Where are you?' It was my dad's voice, and suddenly the shed door opened and there he was. He didn't say anything. He just jerked his thumb over his shoulder, and we reluctantly got up and followed him outside and round the hedge into Angela's drive.

The fire was out and there were huge puddles of water everywhere. All that was left of Uncle Jim's old garage was a wet and blackened shell that sort of steamed gently in the sunshine. The fire engine was still in the street and the firemen were all standing about arguing with Uncle Jim. My dad pushed Angela and me towards them, and everybody turned round and looked at us.

'I think these two young ladies have got some explaining to do,' said my dad sternly.

Well, of course they had found the paraffin can and the box of matches so they knew it hadn't been an accident and we couldn't have denied anything even if we'd wanted to. So when the fire chief asked us if we'd started the fire deliberately we could only nod our heads and stare dumbly at the ground.

Uncle Jim was terribly upset. 'I really can't believe that Angela ...' he began. He stopped and gave me a suspicious look.

'Which one of you is really to blame?' he said.

There was a small silence. Angela gazed up at the sky with a far-away expression in her big blue eyes. Then she looked at me.

'Well,' she said. 'It was actually Charlie who struck the match. Wasn't it, Charlie?'

I scowled at her. But I couldn't deny it because it was true. I thought it was pretty rotten of her to mention it, though, and I could see that my dad thought so too.

'Come off it, Angela,' he said. 'That's not the point. It's not a question of who actually struck the match, and you know it. It's really a question of whose idea it was, isn't it? That's what matters most.'

Angela looked up at my dad and she had a funny look in her eyes as if she was laughing inside. And then you'll never believe what she had the nerve to say.

'In that case, Uncle Ted,' she said, 'it's all your fault. It was you who had the idea in the first place.'

Nobody said anything for a minute. We all just sort of stood there staring at her and she stared back at us with that funny little smile on her face and suddenly I couldn't stand it any longer. And that's when I flew at her and started pulling her hair and kicking her shins and yelling at her and I've never been so mad with Angela in my whole life. And time after time I've taken the blame for things she's done and never complained and I've let her get away with murder because she's my best friend but if she thought I was just going to stand there and let her put the blame on my dad she had another think coming.

'You BEAST!' I shouted. 'How dare you say that! You know he was only making a joke.' And do you know, she was so amazed to see me getting mad that she didn't even try to fight back and I probably would have scratched her eyes out if they hadn't dragged me off her.

Anyway, in the end they decided that we were equally to blame and so we were both sent to our rooms for a whole week. And it was awful because I wasn't allowed out to play or anything and I even had my meals brought up on a tray.

But you can't keep somebody like Angela locked up for long, and on the third night I was suddenly startled by a small shower of pebbles rattling on my bedroom window. I went to open it and there was Angela standing in the flower-bed and she had climbed out and shinned down the drainpipe while her parents were watching the telly. I was still mad with her of course, and I was going to slam the window and refuse to speak to her, but she looked so funny and pathetic standing there in the pouring rain making faces at me and with a great big rip in her pyjamas where she had caught them on a nail; that I couldn't help giggling. And once I had started giggling I somehow couldn't stay mad any more.

So off she went and got the ladder from the shed, and she climbed up to the window and I helped her over the sill. And do you know she was as sorry as anything and she even had a letter of apology to my dad, all nicely done in her very best handwriting. So of course I had to give in and make friends again, and I was glad I did, because she came every night after that and somehow she made being locked up seem like fun.

And Uncle Jim did get round to building a nice new garage in the end, and it looked very smart with the doors painted blue to match the car. I don't know where he got the money from, though, because the insurance company didn't pay for it. The old one wasn't even insured.

II

ONE afternoon towards the end of term we were clearing up the classroom before going home when Miss Bennett made an announcement.

'Listen carefully, everybody,' she said. 'This is your homework for the weekend. I want you each to do a nature project, on any subject you choose, and hand it in on Monday morning.' A few people at the back started groaning, but Miss Bennett held up her hand for silence.

'There will be a small prize for the best one,' she went on, 'but the important thing is that I shall be awarding stars for neatness and presentation, as well as for content.' Miss Bennett gazed round the class over the top of her spectacles.

'It will give you a chance to earn a few more stars before the end of term,' she said sternly. 'Some of you are not doing at all well so far, and I don't have to remind you what that means.'

I wasn't worried, because I already had the most stars for maths, and the most stars for English, and I knew I was going to be near the top of the class anyway. But I felt a bit sorry for Angela. Miss Bennett was staring straight at her as she spoke and it wasn't surprising, because Angela had hardly any stars at all. She'd spent too much time this term larking about when she should have been working, and even that fat lump Laurence Parker had done better than her.

'I'm hoping to see a lot of you pulling your socks up this weekend,' Miss Bennett said. That made me want to giggle. I always want to giggle when teachers say that. Epsecially when it's Miss Bennett, because she wears those sort of brown woolly tights that are always wrinkled around her ankles, so somebody should tell her to do the same.

Well, we all got quite keen and excited and there was a lot of chat about the projects as we came out of school and started walking home. Angela put her arm in mine in ever such a friendly way, so I knew she was going to try and pinch one of my ideas.

'What are you going to do your project on, Charlie?' she asked.

'I don't know yet,' I said. 'I haven't really thought about it.' And it was very strange because that's when it suddenly hit me. We were passing Mrs Harvey's front garden at the time, and she's got this great big buddleia bush, you know the kind I mean, with long clusters of purple flowers a bit like lilac. Well, anyway, the whole bush was simply smothered in butterflies, of all colours and shapes and sizes, and I just stopped dead and stared.

Angela started tugging at my arm. 'Come on, Charlie,' she said. 'What are you gawping at?'

'Butterflies,' I said slowly.

'Pardon?' said Angela.

'Butterflies!' I said. 'A project on butterflies! And caterpillars and chrysalisses and things, and lots of nice drawings, coloured with felt pens. It'll be lovely.' The more I thought about it the more I liked the idea, and I could hardly wait to get started. But Angela was pulling the most awful faces.

'Coo, it'll be lovely!' she mimicked, in a soppy sort of voice. 'Charlie Ellis, you make me sick. Butterflies, pooh! How soft can you get! I'm going to do prehistoric monsters or vampire bats or something like that. Something a bit more exciting than butterflies, anyhow!'

She stalked away and I had to run to catch up with her. 'I think prehistoric monsters is a good idea, too,' I said, to soothe her down. 'But I'm still going to do butterflies.'

Angela shrugged. 'Please yourself,' she said. 'But don't blame me if you get sent all the way back to kindergarten.'

I laughed at that, but it wasn't all that funny really because the end of term marks do count a lot. You see, ours is one of those old-fashioned schools where you are only allowed to go up to the next class if your work is good enough. If it's bad you can even get sent down to the class below, although that's never happened to anybody I know. My mum and dad are always arguing about whether or not it's a good thing, because my mum says it's wrong to make any child feel a failure, but my dad says don't be daft, a bit of hard work and healthy competition never did anybody any harm. But I wonder if he just says that because I always manage to go up. He might feel a bit differently if I ever got sent down.

Anyway, I was dying to start on my butterflies, so when we were going past the paper shop I pulled Angela inside.

'Come on,' I said. 'Let's buy some nice folders to put

our projects in. Miss Bennett is giving extra stars for presentation.'

There were dozens of lovely cardboard folders in the paper shop and it was very hard to choose, but in the end we both picked out a nice blue one. They were the kind with rings in the middle to hold the pages, and they had a neat little transparent plastic pocket on the front where you could slot a bit of card to show your name and the title. I had to pay for Angela's as well, because she'd spent all her pocket money, and they cost me every penny I had left. But they were worth it.

'Come round after tea,' I said to Angela as we parted by her gate. 'We'll go to the library and do some work together, shall we?'

'If you like,' she said. But she didn't sound at all enthusiastic.

And the whole evening turned out to be a disaster, because when we got to the library we found that awful Delilah Jones there as well, AND that fat Laurence Parker, and they'd had the idea of working on their projects, too. Well, that's what they were supposed to be doing. What they were really doing was messing about and giggling and throwing screwed up bits of paper at each other and not getting any work done at all.

Angela went straight over and joined them at their table and I sat by myself in the corner with my back to them and traced some pictures of butterflies from a big book of coloured photographs. But it's very hard to take no notice when people are whispering rude things behind you and flicking bits of paper at the back of your neck. I ignored them as long as I could and I did manage to get a few drawings done, but soon I was giggling just as much as the others and pinging their bits of paper back at them. So of course after a while we all got thrown out by the librarian and it was a bit embarrassing because it was Mrs Woodbridge who is a friend of my mum's and she tutted like anything when she saw me and said 'I'm disappointed in you, Charlie Ellis.'

On the way home I asked Angela if she wanted to come round on Saturday to do some work since she had nothing at all to show for her evening in the library. But she said she was going to her cousin Roger's to play with his new labrador puppies.

'Oh,' I said. 'But when will you do your project?'

'There's stacks of time for that,' said Angela. 'I can do it on Sunday. It won't take me long once I get started.'

On Saturday it poured with rain all day long so I sat indoors at the kitchen table all by myself and worked like mad. At first it was awfully dull and boring without Angela to chat to, but at least it meant that I could get down to some real work for a change and after a while I started to enjoy myself. I wrote an enormous long composition all about the life of the butterfly and where they lay their eggs and I described lots of different sorts of caterpillars and what they feed on and how they spin their cocoons and all that sort of stuff. And then after lunch I heaved out the old second-hand typewriter that my Uncle Barrie gave me last summer when he bought his new electronic one and I carefully typed the whole thing with two fingers on to neat white pages with double spacing between the lines to make it look a lot and when I'd finished it did look jolly impressive.

It was quite late in the evening and I was busy colouring some more butterfly drawings when Angela banged on the back door and walked in. She stared at the typewriter on the kitchen table. Then she picked up my neatly typed composition, took one look at it, and threw it down in disgust.

'You rotten thing! You've typed it!' she said accusingly, as if it was a crime.

'Well, why not?' I said. 'You know my handwriting's awful.'

'But now your project is bound to be the neatest,' she objected.

'No, it isn't,' I said. 'There's nothing to stop you from typing yours, if you want. You've had just as much practice as me. It just takes a long time, that's all.'

So in the end she decided to type hers, too. But she didn't half grumble about it, and I had to help her to carry the heavy typewriter round to her house.

'I won't be seeing you tomorrow,' she said, as I left. 'I suppose I shall have to work all blooming day on this rotten thing.' The way she said it you would have thought it was all my fault, so I thought I'd better not remind her that she'd already wasted most of the weekend. She'd probably have thrown something at me.

The next day was Sunday and the weather had turned warm and sunny. So when I'd finished all my drawings for the project I took my box of water colour paints and a stool and I sat in Mrs Harvey's front garden in the sunshine and started to paint a picture of that buddleia bush all covered in butterflies to stick on the inside front cover. Mrs Harvey likes painting too, and she came out and sat with me for a while and she kept giving me helpful tips and bits of advice and it turned out to be the best painting I've ever done in my life.

I expected Angela to be working too, so I was very surprised when she appeared in the street with her roller skates on. That awful Delilah Jones was with her, and they raised their eyebrows at each other and started to snigger when they spotted me sitting in Mrs Harvey's garden. They came and leaned on the fence and stared and said rude things about me and I felt as uncomfortable as anything.

'What does that look like to you, Delilah?' said Angela, looking at me with her head on one side, as if I was some strange animal in a zoo.

'Looks like some sort of a swot,' said Delilah, wrinkling her nose.

'That's what I think, too,' said Angela. 'Or a teacher's pet, or something horrible like that. Come on, it's not worth looking at.' And off they went, still sniggering.

It was lucky I'd finished my painting by then because what they said made me feel a bit upset. I packed up my things and trailed miserably off home, and I couldn't help wondering if maybe they were right about me, although to be honest I had really enjoyed working on my project and I hadn't done it just to get stars or please the teacher or anything like that.

I stopped worrying about it and soon cheered up when I got home though, because there were freshly picked raspberries with cream for tea and hot scones straight out of the oven and my mum and dad and I sat outside on a rug under the apple tree and there was this lovely smell all around us of new-mown hay because my dad had just finished cutting the lawn.

Then in the evening I finished my project and put it all together. I clipped it into its smart blue folder and showed it to my dad and he said it was smashing and what a clever girl I was. I didn't take too much notice of that because my dad thinks everything I do is smashing and he's convinced I'm going to turn out to be a famous writer or an artist or an Olympic runner or something. I once wrote a silly poem that wasn't even all that funny, and my dad laughed so much that he gave himself a pain in the ribs and had to lie down on the sofa for ten whole minutes. But my mum said the project was very good, too, so I knew it must be all right. My mum only says something is good if it really is.

All I had to do now was to type the label for the front of my folder. But Angela still had my typewriter, so I tucked my project under my arm and walked round to her house. Auntie Sally opened the door.

'Hello, Charlie,' she said. 'Angela's upstairs in her room, wrestling with her homework. I don't know how she expects to get it all done in one evening, but you know what she's like. Always leaves everything until the last minute.'

I went upstairs and tapped on Angela's bedroom door. She gave a sort of groan, so I opened the door and went in. There she was, sitting at that nice leather-topped writing desk of hers, with bits of paper all over the place and torn up drawings and sheets of typing in heaps on the floor.

'Hello,' I said. 'Nearly finished?'

'Well, actually, it's finished,' she said, pushing her fringe away from her hot face. 'But it's pretty awful. Let's have a look at yours.'

'Wait a minute till I do the title,' I said. I popped my small square of thin white card into the typewriter and carefully typed 'Butterflies. By Charlie Ellis.' Then I slipped the card into the little plastic pocket on the front of the folder so that it showed through. Angela took it from me with a scowl.

'It looks awfully thick,' she said. 'What've you done, written a book?' I saw what she meant when I compared it with hers. She'd only done about four pages, and she hadn't even managed to do those neatly. The typing was all messy, with a lot of rubbing out and mistakes and there was even a hole in the paper in one place where she'd rubbed right through. I could see quite a few places where she hadn't bothered to check her spelling, and the drawings were terrible. Angela's cousin Dominic could have done better, and he's only five and a half.

But the thing that really surprised me was the title of the project. I kept staring at the front of the folder because I just couldn't believe it after all she'd said. 'Butterflies,' it said. 'By Angela Mitchell.'

I wanted to ask her about that but I didn't get a chance because it was then that she flung my project on the floor and started shouting and it was horrible because I never know what to do when she gets furious like that and this time she was madder than I've ever seen her before.

'You rotten CREEP!' she yelled. 'You've already got more stars than anybody else, but that's not enough, is it? All you care about is being top of the class. You don't care about me at all, do you. Well, it doesn't bother me, I can tell you. You can jolly well go up to Miss Bridge's class next term without me and we'll never be friends again. Never ever!'

She pushed me out of her bedroom and slammed the door. I stood there for a little while and I didn't know what to do because I didn't feel like knocking on the door and asking for my project back. But just then the door was pulled open and my folder came sailing out and bounced along the landing. I picked it up and hurried off home before she decided to do something worse.

That night I could hardly sleep. All the things Angela had said kept going round and round in my head, and I couldn't think of anything I could do to put things right. It wasn't my fault that she'd done such a rotten piece of work, but even if I didn't hand mine in it wouldn't make hers any better. And it would be awful to go up to Miss Bridge's without her. She might be a bit rotten to me sometimes, but she's such fun to be with, and I knew I'd be as bored as anything if she wasn't my friend.

I was still thinking about it the next morning on my way to school. Angela didn't speak to me at all and I felt miserable. It was only after we'd all handed in our projects and Miss Bennett had arranged them on a long table at the back of the classroom that I had a sudden crazy idea. It was probably a very wicked thing to do, but it was the only way I could think of to help Angela get more stars. I thought about it carefully, and I knew it would work. It would be cheating, but cheating for the sake of somebody else is not nearly as bad as cheating for yourself. Well, that's what I think, anyway.

So, at break time, when everybody else dashed out to the playground, I hung around for a minute or two until the classroom was empty. I went to the back of the room where the projects were and I stood in front of the table with my heart going thump thump inside me. I found the two blue folders that were Angela's and mine, and I slipped both our name cards out of the little plastic pockets. Then I swapped them round, so that Angela's name was on my folder, and mine was on hers. Once I nearly died when I thought I heard Miss Bennett coming back, but nobody caught me, and I escaped outside as fast as I could.

In the playground I started looking around for Angela and that nice David Watkins told me that she'd just gone inside by the other door. I thought I'd go and look for her, because I wanted to try to make friends, so I went down the corridor to our classroom to see if she was there. She was there all right, doing something at the project table. She turned round quickly when I said her name and her face went sort of a funny colour.

'What are you doing, following me around?' she snapped. Then she suddenly became all smiles. 'Sorry, Charlie,' she said. 'I'm being horrible to you, aren't I.' She came over to me and put her arm through mine. 'Come on, Charlie,' she said. 'Let's be friends.' And we went out arm in arm, with me feeling so pleased that I completely forgot to wonder what she had been up to with those project folders.

I soon found out, though. It was at the end of the afternoon when the projects had been marked and Miss Bennett was getting ready to announce the winner. We all sat there as quiet as mice and I couldn't wait to see Angela's face if Miss Bennett called out her name.

My heart missed a beat as Miss Bennett held up a blue folder. 'First prize,' she said, with a big beam on her face, 'goes to Charlotte Ellis, for a delightful piece of work on butterflies.'

Well, I was stunned. I sat there, blinking and opening and shutting my mouth, and I couldn't think what could have gone wrong. Miss Bennett opened the folder and began to show the class some of the drawings, and the painting of the buddleia bush, so I knew it was my project all right. But how had it got my name on it?

And then I looked over my shoulder at Angela, and you should have seen her face. She was livid. But she was also just as amazed as I was, and that's how I knew. That's when I realized just what it was she had been doing in the classroom that morning. She'd been swapping the names on the folders, thinking she was getting mine. And all the time she'd been getting her own rotten one back again!

I suppose I should have felt sorry for Angela, but it was her own silly fault, after all, and I couldn't do anything but laugh. I was laughing all the time I collected my prize and my three gold stars and everybody started clapping and I felt as proud as anything.

And everything worked out all right in the end, because Miss Bennett gave Angela such a good talking to about her work that she actually did manage to pull her socks up a bit before we broke up for the summer and she just managed to scrape through the end of term tests.

So we're going up together next term to Miss Bridge's after all, and we're still the best of friends. And the funny thing is that Angela is a lot nicer to me now than she used to be. She treats me with a kind of respect, almost.

'You were too clever for me that time, Charlie Ellis,' she said with a grin, and there was a sort of admiration in her voice.

I still don't know what she thinks I did. But I've never told her what really happened, and I don't think I ever will.